Don't you wish you'd learned years ago how to say no in a caring and honoring way? With her personal experiences and the truth of God's Word as her blueprint, Karen has created a valuable resource to guide the approval addict out of a life stifled by misery.

—CHRYSTAL EVANS HURST, bestselling author and speaker

Karen offers ways to put your people-pleasing tendencies in perspective so you can experience the freedom and happiness you deserve. This book is a great guide to help you break free from the toxic patterns of pleasing others at the risk of losing yourself.

—REBEKAH LYONS, bestselling author of
Rhythms of Renewal and *You Are Free*

I'm so grateful to Karen Ehman for writing a book on the much-needed topic of people pleasing. As someone who has struggled with being miserable, anxious, and stressed over what people think about me, I constantly need reminders of the truth that it's not my job to win the approval of others but to instead honor the Lord with my life.

—CRYSTAL PAINE, *New York Times* bestselling author,
podcaster, and founder of MoneySavingMom.com

Karen Ehman's books are always practical, purposeful, and firmly rooted in Scripture. This one is all that and more. Digging deep into her own people-pleasing heart, Karen mines priceless gems that sparkle with truth. And, like diamonds, those hard truths cut through our resistance to change, helping us focus on pleasing God rather than people. Her best book yet.

—LIZ CURTIS HIGGS, bestselling author of *The Girl's Still Got It*

If the people pleaser in you is allowing others to pull you apart at the seams, this book will help put you back together again! In Karen Ehman's new book, you will encounter the good news of God's approval of us in Christ—an approval that will enable you to love others, in time, deeply and freely.

—DR. PATRICK SCHWENK, pastor, cohost of the Rootlike Faith
podcast, and coauthor of *In a Boat in the Middle of a Lake*

This book should be required reading for every woman! Karen is masterful at moving from biblical principles to practical application, and she doesn't leave any area of the people-pleasing trap untouched within these pages. Get ready for a real conversation you may not even realize you need to have.

—MICHELLE MYERS, founder of She Works HIS Way

Within the first chapter I felt like Karen was inside my head: *How does she know my thoughts?* Anyone struggling with people pleasing and approval addiction will feel known by this book—and not just known but led closer to Christ: our savior and ultimate Approver.

—PHYLICIA MASONHEIMER, founder and
CEO of Every Woman a Theologian

Through pointed stories, sound theology, and practical advice, Karen offers insight and refreshing vulnerability. You'll laugh. You'll gulp. And as you journey *with her* through the process of exposing people pleasing, you'll rejoice in finding a way forward. May this hopeful book help you replace needless misery with God's boundless acceptance!

—JUSTIN DETMERS, PhD, Riverview
Church, REO Town Venue pastor

This book left me feeling convicted in the best way. Karen gives you tools, backed by Scripture, on how to stop living your life at the mercy of others so you can start building a life that pleases God. She teaches you how to say no with confidence so you can live a life less stressed and more fulfilled in the long run.

—AMBER EMILY SMITH, wife of country music artist Granger
Smith, mother, actor, philanthropist, and influencer

In these pages, Ehman uses insights from God's Word to pinpoint precisely why we struggle with people pleasing, as well as to provide simple steps for living free. If you cannot stop craving approval, this book has good news for you.

—SHARON HODDE MILLER, author of *Nice: Why We
Love to Be Liked and How God Calls Us to More*

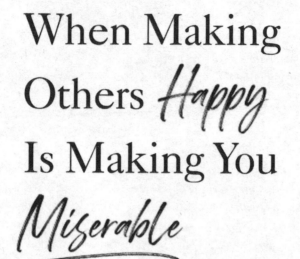

When Making
Others *Happy*
Is Making You
Miserable

When Making Others *Happy* Is Making You *Miserable*

HOW TO BREAK THE PATTERN
OF PEOPLE PLEASING AND
CONFIDENTLY LIVE YOUR LIFE

KAREN EHMAN

ZONDERVAN
BOOKS

ZONDERVAN BOOKS

When Making Others Happy Is Making You Miserable
Copyright © 2021 by Karen Ehman

Requests for information should be addressed to:
Zondervan, 3900 Sparks Dr. SE, Grand Rapids, Michigan 49546

Zondervan titles may be purchased in bulk for educational, business, fundraising, or sales promotional use. For information, please email SpecialMarkets@Zondervan.com.

ISBN 978-0-310-34758-3 (softcover)
ISBN 978-0-310-34763-7 (audio)
ISBN 978-0-310-34759-0 (ebook)

Cover design: Alison Fargason Design
Cover photo: Jamie Grill Atlas / Stocksy
Interior design: Denise Froehlich

Printed in the United States of America

21 22 23 24 25 /LSC/ 10 9 8 7 6 5 4 3 2 1

To Ruth and Pat

For the ways you please God and love people

Contents

Foreword by
Lysa TerKeurst

I would love to say that I don't struggle with keeping others happy so I can feel happy. But, sadly, that's not true. I remember the first time someone labeled my struggle as "people pleasing." I was caught off guard and quite honestly offended.

I love people really well. I mean they know they can count on me day and night. It makes me feel awful to say no. It makes me feel great to be the one who says yes! I know I'm a little tired but as long as I'm doing this from a good heart—it's good, right?!

And it was that very misguided thought process that proved how much I needed a wise friend like Karen to help me make some changes.

In Matthew 22:37–39 (NIV), we find some of Jesus' most popular words:

> "Jesus replied: 'Love the Lord your God with all your heart and with all your soul and with all your mind.' This is the first and greatest commandment. And the second is like it: 'Love your neighbor as yourself.'"

Love God. Love people.

Karen has helped me realize that there is a priority in this instruction.

Priority is what I've been missing. For years I've said yes to requests even when I didn't have the capacity or the desire to do what others were asking of me. And if I'm really honest, it often wasn't purely out of love for people that I would stretch myself way too thin. It was because I couldn't figure out how to manage the fear of what disappointing them would cost me. So, constantly trying to win the approval of others left me feeling empty and exhausted.

And that's when my friend Karen helped me reorient my priorities. It's not "love people so that they reassure you that you are loved." No, it's first "love God" and live from that assured place that you are already loved. Then from that confident and compassionate state of mind, "love people" in appropriate ways that don't hyperextend yourself constantly.

You're in safe company if you find yourself in this same struggle. Karen is warm and hilarious and inviting and oh so tenderhearted. But she loves you too much to let you stay in a place where making other people happy is making you miserable.

Let's be honest about what this is really costing us.

Let's admit how it might be taking the best of us away from those who should be a priority.

Let's acknowledge how helpless we feel when we've overcommitted time and time again.

Let's dare to be brave enough to make changes.

Let's rise up and model how healthy it is to break away from pleasing people so we can truly love people without a hidden agenda.

And let's learn to have enough space and quiet and calm to totally step into our one glorious life and truly live.

Chapter 1

The Prison of
People Pleasing

Spotted on a sweatshirt:
"You can't please everyone. You're not pizza."

Am I now trying to win the approval of human
beings, or of God? Or am I trying to please
people? If I were still trying to please people, I
would not be a servant of Christ.
—GALATIANS 1:10

I grabbed a handful of tissues and dashed out the sliding glass
door that leads to our back deck. It was a muggy, Midwest afternoon in late May. My body would have much rather been inside in
the frosty air conditioning, however my mind desperately needed
to escape. To somewhere. Anywhere. And since my son was using
my vehicle to go to work that day, I couldn't go very far.

I plopped myself down in a lawn chair at the wooded portion
of our back property near our fire pit. I'd sat in that bright blue

chair through hundreds of baseball games, cheering my sons on as they were stepping up to the plate to bat or perched on pitcher's mound ready to hurl a curveball. Perhaps now I could cheer *myself* up. But I doubted it. Nothing about my situation—or my near future—looked even remotely cheery to me.

My best friend from college and I had just wrapped up a phone call. We've been in each other's lives for over a quarter century, and she continually has my best interests at heart. A chat with her is a delight in my day, a major pick-me-up. In fact, once we finish, I'll hang up and think, Man. *Talking to her is almost better than church.* We've processed life together since we were both teenagers. We've prayed for each other's marriages, shared our mothering mishaps, and navigated how best to help our aging parents. We offer each other encouragement and advice or simply listen to the other share something trivial, laughing while on speaker phone as we each frantically try to get supper on the table.

But this phone call was different. Although my friend didn't know it, when we ended the call, I wasn't feeling cheered-up or churched-up at all. I was feeling utterly defeated and emotionally exhausted. Oh, it wasn't something she'd said that sent me to this dismal place. Not at all. Well, then what *had* sent me over the edge, threatening to drain the happiness from my heart and send fretfulness filling my soul? It was something I had done dozens . . . maybe hundreds . . . oh come on let's be honest, probably thousands of times . . .

I had said yes.

Our family had moved to a tiny town just outside Lansing, capital of my home state of Michigan. Her college-aged son was in the process of interviewing for a summer internship at an organization in the city. She'd called to inform me that he'd just accepted a position and would soon be working just down the interstate, about fifteen minutes from our new home. The job description fit him to a T, and he was pumped about starting soon.

However, this job was going to require more than an hour commute each way from his home near Detroit. Most days it wouldn't be a problem, as he'd be working a typical nine-to-five-ish day. However, some days he would be responsible for staying late and closing up, getting home near midnight—yet he would still need to be up for work at o'dark o'clock the next morning. Knowing this would be the occasional situation for him—maybe a day or two a week—she asked if he could spend the night with us on those nights, sleeping in our guestroom.

Now, this guy was no trouble at all. We've known him his entire life. He was loads of fun, utterly respectful, and kind. So, who he was had exactly zero to do with a little conversation that commenced inside my mind. This convo was between "outward" me and "inward" me. It is a discussion that my brain has hosted gazillions of times. Here's how it went that day:

> **Inward me:** Oh no. I'm not sure about this. I think we have too much going on this summer to have an overnight guest stay a couple days each week. I should say no.
>
> **Outward me:** But if you say no, you'll disappoint your friend who is just wanting a little help for her son.
>
> **Inward me:** I know, but it just doesn't feel right. I have so much on my plate both at home and in my ministry. I should say no.
>
> **Outward me:** But if you say no, you're also going to let down your friend's son as well. That is *two* people you will disappoint. Besides, he's such a great guy. You should help him out. He won't be any trouble at all.

Inward me: I know how I am. I'll want to make sure his room has clean sheets and fresh towels and I'll stay up at night until he gets here and make him something to eat before he goes to bed. Although I usually love being hospitable, this is going to stress me right out.

Outward me: Oh, come on! You are the master multitasker. You can juggle a myriad of things at once. This one little addition won't be a big deal. Just shuffle some things around on that big ole' plate of yours. You can make it all fit.

Inward me: Oh dear. My mind is starting to race and my heart's beating faster. I'm still dealing with the death of my dad. And my stepmom, mother-in-law, and mother—who are all getting up there in age—sometimes need my help. And we have a new house that we still are remodeling. In fact, the guest room is piled high with wood planks for the new floors that won't get installed for weeks. And I'm a brand-new mother-in-law. I need to carve out time to spend with my new daughter. Oh, and I almost forgot! A family friend just texted a few days ago to ask if they can stay at our house some weekends to help jump-start a new career as a personal shopper by picking up some clients in the city. I'd already answered yes to that request. Oh, *what* was I thinking? How am I ever going to manage all of this?

Outward me: Girlfriend, chill out! You can totally handle it. What you *cannot* handle is failing to accommodate your friend. That will feel way worse than being stressed. Now listen, you have a choice:

It's either disappoint her or slightly inconvenience yourself. You know the right answer. Just say yes.

Inward me: I shouldn't.

Outward me: You must.

Inward me: I really shouldn't.

Outward me: Oh, but you must.

Inward me: No, I'm pretty certain I shouldn't.

Outward me: Oh, stopping kidding yourself, you know that you will!

And then outward me opened wide her big mouth, and let out a resounding, "Sure. No problem!"

Meanwhile, inwardly, my spirit deflated just as quickly as my stress level skyrocketed. And so I ended the call, mumbling something about needing to switch over the laundry. Instead, I left the laundry untouched, reached for some antacids to remedy my ever-growing ulcer, and headed outside to BAWL. MY. FREAKIN'. EYES. OUT.

How Did I Get Here?

Few people are completely immune from people pleasing. The majority of us have said something we didn't really mean, just because we didn't want to hurt someone else's feelings. You know, when your friend asked you what you thought of her new trendy, neon-blue jumpsuit that she was simply crazy about, but that you thought was about two sizes too small and made her look like an overstuffed Smurf? Inwardly you may have thought it was closer to awful than awesome, but you summoned a smile and out of your mouth tumbled a counterfeit compliment, "Wow! It looks so great!"

Why do we say things we don't really mean? It isn't limited

to our desire to avoid hurting someone's feelings. On many occasions, it is wound up in our longing to be liked. Who among us, if we were still in high school and faced with a choice between being an outstanding athlete yet having zero friends or an utter klutz on the field but the recipient of the homecoming crown, would go for the star-athlete status? (Excuse me please while I straighten my tiara.)

Most of us have adopted the practice of saying or doing that which placates others in order to keep conflict at bay. Or we may not speak honestly due to a suspicion that we might be challenged. And how about this one? We simply don't feel like being bothered right now and, if we just agree with them, maybe they will go delightfully away.

All legit reasons, for sure. However, sometimes it goes much deeper.

We might fib just a tad to a superior at work so that they will have a favorable view of us—especially if our potential rise in the company is something on which they have input. Or maybe it is birthed out of earnest sympathy. When someone has experienced repeated disappointments or walked through a dire tragedy, to avoid adding to their sadness, we don't say anything that might upset them. Perhaps the most serious scenario is this: someone caught in a domestic abuse situation. Such an individual will say what their abuser wants to hear, regardless of what they really think or feel. They cannot risk upsetting the abusive person, so they take the brunt of their anger.[1]

When you drill down to unearth the causes of people pleasing, you discover that it isn't just the response of the person we're hoping to make happy that causes us to give in and placate. For some of us, it is a result of how we are hardwired—a product of our particular personality. Although I won't go deep into specific personality tests and theories since there are oodles of great works available (see my favorites in the resource section on page 191), I do think some commonalities exist when it comes to the type of person who is in danger of becoming addicted to the approval of others.

She may be the helpful sort, with kindness in her heart and the most patient of personalities. She truly enjoys assisting others. It's second nature for such a woman to step over a line and help beyond what is healthy or needful.

Another category of persons that may make themselves quite miserable while making others happy are the overachievers among us. Being universally liked and admired can seem like an accomplishment that we—yes, I am talking in plural here because I am 100 percent this type—simply must achieve.

Let's not leave out the perfectionists. These people can feel the tug toward appeasing and satisfying others because they view doing so as the right thing to do. They can rack up a long streak of making others smile without ever missing a beat.

And while we're at it, let's toss all the peacemakers into the mix. (Gently now, for they are sensitive and tenderhearted souls.) Peacemakers can't bear to see anyone upset. They hate the feeling of conflict or the unease of tension hanging in the air. If saying something they really don't mean—or doing something they really don't want to do—will help to keep the peace and pacify someone else, then that is how they'll roll.

Though our reasons and our personalities may vary, there is one universal result that we see from our constant stream of yeses. It is this: trying to make (or keep) others happy often results in making us miserable.

You know the feeling. You said yes to the responsibility, agreed to the task, feigned excitement when you really felt dread, and now your mind races with regret and wishes it could rewind time, going back to the day when your lips said yes when they should have uttered a big fat no! But would revisiting the situation, with a chance for a do-over, really make any difference? After all, you've grown so accustomed to pleasing others that you've stitched a perpetual pattern of pleasing into the very fabric of your life. Smile and say yes when you'd rather say no; totally agree when what you really believe is quite the opposite. Don't ruffle feathers. Don't make them drop their smile. Behave as they desire, regardless of what you really want—or even what you desperately need.

The Longing to Be Liked

The gymnasium at the big brick elementary school in my neighborhood was the site of many activities. We not only marched there for Friday afternoon physical education class, it doubled as our school cafeteria and tripled as our auditorium. (It should have been dubbed the "caf-e-gym-a-torium!") One day I might be up against the wall hoping to get picked early for a dodgeball team. Another day, I might be standing on a riser, singing alongside classmates at a school Christmas concert or spring recital. But most often, it was the place where I munched on my lunch five times a week.

Who among us doesn't remember standing nervously with our lunch tray scanning the room for a place to sit? Such a mental flashback can still stir a sense of anxiety. There's no greater setup for a feeling of rejection or, at the very least, a sense of loneliness. But I didn't fret about sitting alone because I had a secret weapon in my back pocket. Well actually, she was behind the serving table, scooping up mashed potatoes and gravy with a smile. It was my mother, the beloved Delta Center Elementary School lunch lady.

In the cafeteria, if I wanted to win friends—and influence enemies—Mom was just the ticket. In addition to our basic scoops and mounds of food piled high on our rectangular pastel plastic trays, we had the option of purchasing an ice cream sand-wich for a mere fifteen cents. My mom would often treat me to one, along with whatever friend I happened to be sitting with that day. Naturally, lots of people wanted to be my friend. I mean, who doesn't love a chocolate-cookie-covered slab of icy vanilla cream-iness? (Grabs phone to add "ice cream sandwiches" to her app grocery list.)

It was this kind gesture by my mother that taught me an important life lesson: make someone happy and then they will like you. And since my single-digit-year-old self didn't relish the feeling of not being liked, I resolved to never let that happen, if it were within my power. Gifting a fellow classmate with a frozen dairy confection wasn't my only tool for maintaining friendships. My behavior in other areas ensured that I would feel wanted and loved. I dished out compliments I really didn't mean, nodded in agreement just so as not to bring any tension or create any conflict, and, of course, I joined forces with mean girls who didn't like someone else in our class. I had to. What if I didn't and the mean girls all turned on me?

I soon became an approval junkie—longing for belonging, addicted to acceptance, craving the calm of no tension in a con-versation, and the security that being liked seemed to bring my young soul. But here is the thing about living like this . . .

To keep it up, you have to become a skillful liar.

Yes, you heard me. People pleasers are also deceivers. We do not always speak the truth. We shade it. Skirt it. Dress it up just a tad before taking it for a spin. Or—worst of all—we leave truth completely out of the picture.

When asked what we think of lying, we "yes girls" will assert that lying is wrong. After all, isn't the Bible bursting with warn-ings about the sin of shading the truth? But take a good look at our lives and a different reality materializes. Often, on occasions of people pleasing, we do not tell the truth. It was a colossal wake-up call for me the day I admitted this reality. That aha moment helped to put me on the path to becoming a recovering people pleaser. Notice I said *recovering*, as in present tense. I have not arrived, nor will I ever. Learning to deal with this relational issue is a tension to manage. It's not a problem that can suddenly be solved with a snap of the fingers. (But oh sister, do I ever wish it were!)

Guess what else people pleasing does to us? Although it may gain us a reputation for being helpful and competent, it also creates a ton more work for us. Is that not totally true?

In what ways has appeasing others made more work for you? Did you stay up late to bake a ton of brownies for your child's soccer team, even though you were low on sleep and had an extremely busy week, when there were tons of other soccer moms who hadn't made a solitary sweet yet this season? Did you agree to go mow the yard for your aging grandparents nearly every week in the summer, even though you have a half-dozen cousins who could easily have taken a turn? (But you didn't want to speak up and suggest that they give you a break.) Are you the only one who ever cleans out the coffee maker at work and—now that you have been doing it so long—people expect it of you even though they themselves are perfectly capable? And so, you just keep on serving as the designated breakroom butler.

The work we create for ourselves isn't limited to physical work. We also make more emotional work for ourselves—draining, exhaustive, and exasperating emotional work. I've had feelings of regret for the things I agreed to do that I really didn't want to do, or that I even strongly felt God would *not* have me to do. I deal with anger at times when I get a sneaking feeling that I am being used or taken advantage of. I experience deep despondency when I feel powerless to break the habit of taking on tasks that others could easily do themselves. But most of all, it's the overall feeling of emotional exhaustion that blankets my mind as I juggle the responsibilities and tasks I have added to my own plate simply to be liked and approved of. And I replay the scenarios of these draining decisions over and over in my mind, imagining what I could have—and should have—done differently.

Our inward selves—deep in the secret conversations of our minds—really are able to come up with all sorts of ways to say no. To politely decline. To not volunteer once again. To let the person who is pouting just keep on pouting, rather than agreeing to something they want us to do. Yes, in our minds we may have riveting reasons and logical explanations that could finally result in some straightforward and honest living. The trouble is, our approval-addicted outward selves just can't seem to send the proper message.

People pleasing brings such detriment to our lives. We make ourselves miserable. We lie. We create more work for ourselves— both physical and emotional work. We lose grasp of our joy. We offer a standing invitation to regret. This is all so profoundly discouraging. But do you know what is the absolute worst of all?

When we behave this way, we are putting people in the place of God.

OUCH!

My Summer of Necessary and No

A few days later, I found myself again in a lawn chair at our fire pit on an early evening. The heaving of my chest slowly subsided as I began to calm down and finish up my latest spontaneous crying session. As I stared up at the slices of sunlight slashing through the dancing branches of the towering maple trees, I poured my heart out to the Lord about the phone call with my college best friend. Of course, he already knew the whole story, including the predictable outcome of my saying yes when I should have said no. Still, it felt good to verbalize my inner thoughts to God. I just hoped no one else heard me, except for the half dozen or so black squirrels that reside in the trees and pass time by stealing the birdseed from our feeders. After all, the neighbors, who were simply trying to eat their supper in peace, didn't need both dinner *and* a show.

My phone was next to me on a small table. I reached for it and logged on to an app for reading the Bible and locating passages. I swiped my way to the passage look-up page and then tapped away, placing two words in the search bar: *please people.* Just a millisecond after clicking the little magnifying glass that set the search in motion, twenty-three verses appeared before my eyes. I read them. Some didn't apply to my situation, although they had both words in the passage. But when I spied entry number twenty-two, it was as if it were flashing in neon pink, its words penetrating straight to my soul.

The apostle Paul wrote a New Testament letter to the early church in Galatia, an area that is part of modern-day Turkey. Though it was composed between 53 and 57 AD, its message still has great relevance today. A good chunk of Galatians deals with the pressure the early Christians there felt from a group known as the Judaizers. Members of this group were insisting that converts to Christianity still follow some practices in the Old Testament law, asserting that it was necessary to do so to be a true believer and obtain salvation. Paul corrected this notion, reminding everybody of the true gospel of Christ that offers us salvation by trusting him alone, the one who paved the way to heaven through his death on the cross in our place (Galatians 1:6–7; 3:26).

At the onset of this message to the Galatians, Paul tosses out an important question. It's a question I've learned to ask myself often. I so wish I could say I always give the right answer. Sadly, I don't. But I am getting better, and I know you can too!

What is this question? Here it goes: "Am I now trying to win the approval of human beings, or of God? Or am I trying to please people? If I were still trying to please people, I would not be a servant of Christ" (Galatians 1:10).

Hold up! Pause the video! Wait—what! People in Bible days struggled with people pleasing? I mean weren't they all perfect, running around donning halos that would rival the most glorious Instagram filter and singing the latest worship songs they'd just downloaded from their Spiritual Spotify app?

Nope. They dealt with this interpersonal tension in their life just like we do. And we would do well to ponder Paul's question today when we are trapped in a tug of war between following God and succumbing to pressure from people.

I scanned the verse over and over again, committing its convicting question and relevant phrases to memory. "Am I now trying to win the approval of human beings, or of God? Or am I trying to please people? If I were still trying to please people, I would not be a servant of Christ."

However, I knew that rote memorization was not the entire key. I needed not only to sear the words in my mind, but I needed to take them to heart; to allow them to alter my behavior and—although I didn't know it at the time—revolutionize my relationships.

Over the next few days, I talked to God and dug into his Word. It was then that I sensed him leading me to do something quite out of the ordinary, something I had never done before. I ran the idea by my husband, and he was beyond supportive. In fact, he'd been wanting me to do something like this for years. What was the idea? It was really very simple. I sensed God telling me this: *"Sweetheart, I'm calling you to have a summer of 'necessary' and 'no.'"*

Here was the idea: For the next three months, until Labor Day,

I was to do only the things necessary for my work, my home, and my family. Nothing else. No outside guests. No offering to watch someone's children. No solving other people's problems. No signing up for even simple things like making treats for the childcare kids to snack on during church worship services. No saying yes to even wonderfully good things, like attending a Bible study with a friend. I was to do only what was necessary and say no to the rest.

I know that might sound rather severe. However, it was to be my first real break in over twenty-five years of my adult life. Twenty. Five. Years. Yikes! Even way back in late high school when I first met Jesus and began to follow him, I was guilty not only of people pleasing, but also of over-serving. You could count on me to be the first one to raise my hand to help. To offer to set up or clean up—or sometimes, if needed, to do both! To prepare the food or watch the kiddos in the church nursery. To run the errand and lighten the load. To look oh-so-capable and really quite wonderful. But after a quarter century, I needed a break—something fierce.

I then knew what was next on this new assignment. Make a few phone calls. Send some text messages. I needed to cancel some things. Drop out of some things. To take back some things I'd said. Basically, I needed to bulldoze my calendar for the glorious fourteen weeks that comprised the summer ahead, leaving only the important stuff standing. I knew it was going to be excruciatingly painful for this "what-does-it-look-like-to-everyone-regardless-of-what-it-is-doing-to-me" kind of gal. Still, I swallowed hard and grabbed my phone.

I wish I could say everyone on the other end of the line took it fantastically; that they understood how much I needed a break and insinuated that it was well deserved. But this just wasn't so. Some were simply cordial but slightly hard to read. I wasn't sure if they were upset with me or just bummed because they then had to implement a back-up plan. A few did cheerfully declare,

"No problem!" and were supportive of my decision. Others guilt-bombed me, albeit stealthily, implying that they were going to be inconvenienced by my no longer agreeing to cheerfully meet one of their needs.

And then there was my last call to make—to my college best friend. I knew calling her would be the hardest since I was the closest to her, with years and years of friendship behind—and before—us. My saying yes to her request would have really helped out her son, who needed an occasional place to stay during his internship. I was sorry I was about to disappoint her.

I hauled myself back out to the fire pit, confident in the fact that the squirrels were now quite accustomed to my incessant sobbing, so it wouldn't bother them any if I blubbered again. (I half expected them to summon the cardinals and blue jays, who would fly through the air and gently float me down a hanky held between their beaks. You know, like Cinderella or Snow White's little forest friends would do?) I swiped my phone screen on and dialed her number. (Yes, I said, "dialed." She's had the same number for a couple decades, and I know it by heart. That is how close we are.)

I mostly held it together as I relayed my dilemma to her, apologizing for saying yes when I knew in my heart the answer should have been no. My friend loves me, and I was confident she would be understanding, although probably a bit disappointed. However, I was not fully prepared for the onslaught of love—and the clear reflection of Jesus—that materialized as I heard her voice coming through my phone.

This normally soft-spoken and quiet woman piped up, "Listen, Kit" (my college nickname, in case you didn't know), "it's totally okay. Don't even think another thing about it. We'll figure something out. What I'm more concerned about is you, and your health. Get some rest and we can talk in a week or so. I'm going to be checking in on you throughout the summer."

As we continued talking, the twisted-up tension began to slowly unknot from my shoulders. My soul simmered down, and my emotions quieted. Her genuine concern for me was what was most evident. There wasn't even a hint of disappointment in her voice.

She herself had recently been through a stretch of a few years when she dealt with a loved one who was suffering from stress, anxiety, and near burnout, sometimes leaving them unable to work. Her experience watching this person navigate an emotionally tumultuous time packed her heart with empathy and understanding. Her gracious response to me enabled me to sleep deeply and soundly for the first time in over a week. And it assured me that those in my life who love me—and want me to follow God—will understand when I make a decision that is not the most advantageous for them. Her kindness that day was the greatest of gifts.

How about you? Have your people-pleasing tendencies landed you in a heap of heartache, at least a time or two? Are you tired of outwardly agreeing to something that inwardly you're certain you shouldn't? Does trying to keep everyone happy end up making you quite the opposite? Are you in desperate need of your own season of necessary and no? And—if you're completely honest—would you admit that sometimes you put people in the place of God?

If any of these questions spark even a slight yes in your heart, I invite you to join me on this pathway I am still learning to walk. I'm just a few steps up ahead, navigating my way but finding the hike less scary—and less difficult—as it becomes more and more familiar. Like a muscle that must be exercised but grows stronger over time, your ability to discern and decide what pleases God, rather than people, will sharpen as you move forward in your own walk with Jesus.

Head out with me now to my little maple grove. There we will sit together by the fire as we also learn to sit at his feet. A black squirrel or two may join us. Maybe even some of our colorful, feathered friends. But soon the sun will slice through the shade of the leaves as the Son helps disperse the darkness that we experience due to our people-pleasing ways.

Together we will learn to walk closely—and confidently— with our loving Creator, despite the opinions and expectations of others.

Quiz: What Is Your Approval Rating?

Often, we may catch a news report that gives a politician's approval rating. This is the result of a poll taken to determine what percentage of the people surveyed are satisfied with the job the person is doing. Time for us to take our own poll. However, this one has a slightly different twist.

Read through the following statements and note the number that best describes you, using the key below. Then, total up the numbers to see where you fall on the approval rating scale.

5	4	3	2	1
Never	Rarely	Sometimes	Usually	Always

1. I have trouble expressing my honest opinion when someone asks me what I think of their outfit, hair, new shoes, etc. . . . ___2___

2. If I'm in a group deciding where to eat and the majority of people have already weighed in wanting restaurant A but I want restaurant B, I will just go along with their choice rather than tell them the truth. ___1___

3. In a group setting where a leader is asking for volunteers for a task, I will make sure to be one of the people to sign up to do a job or provide food. __1__

4. I am hypersensitive to being corrected by others. __2__

5. I second-guess myself when I start to wonder what someone else might think of my decision. __1__

6. When people, especially strangers, are talking about politics—and are on the opposite side of what I feel is an important moral issue—I will just keep my opinions to myself rather than tell them what I believe. __2__

7. I get uncomfortable even with the illusion of dissatisfaction from others. __2__

8. When in a group setting and asked to give my opinion, when I'm finished talking, I hope others will chime in and agree with me. __2__

9. If you looked at my life, you would characterize me as someone who is overcommitted. __1__

10. When I meet someone new, I hope that after our encounter they like me. __1__

11. I fear being exposed for my real thoughts because I might be considered an imposter. __3__

12. If I am being totally honest, I have to admit that there are times I lie because I fear getting a negative reaction from someone else, and so I say what I know they want to hear. __4__

13. I might want to speak up and say something that does not please a person with whom I am talking, but I am afraid of losing them as a friend. __2__

14. I don't have trouble expressing my honest opinions with my immediate family members, who already love me, but I do have trouble expressing opinions to someone outside my family who has the option of liking me or not. ___2___
15. If I sense that someone does not like me, it bothers me. ___2___
16. A person who knows me on a surface level would say I am an extremely reliable and helpful person. ___2___
17. I have a strong desire for verbal praise, whether spoken or written digitally in an email, text message, or on social media. ___2___
18. I say yes to some things that create more work for me rather than say no and risk disappointing or upsetting the person doing the asking. ___1___
19. I give compliments I do not really mean. ___2___
20. My desire to make others happy ends up making me at least slightly miserable. ___2___

Grand Total: ___37___

Alright. How did you do? Let's see where your grand total places you.

81–100: You really don't sabotage your life by being an immense people pleaser. Good for you! You will still benefit from this book; however, you might want to pass it on to a major people pleaser when you're finished reading, because you most likely won't have to refer to it again—but they might need to read it yearly!

61–80: You are probably about average on the people-pleasing scale. Sometimes you fall into this tendency, but other times you are completely comfortable expressing your honest opinion and not being overcommitted. Bravo! Although you definitely have room for improvement, more of us need to be like you.

41–60: People pleasing and being addicted to the approval of others is a minor problem in your life. You probably struggle with it when it comes to certain people but not when it comes to others. You can learn to make progress, fearing less and less what certain people think.

31–40: Yep. Approval addiction is definitely an issue for you. Most likely it has caused you grief and sadness, but you can't seem to stop doing it. Buckle up, honey. We've got some changes to make.

21–30: Welcome to the "Make Them Happy!" club, of which I am a charter member. People like us. They really like us! They think we're capable. And so helpful. Our schedules are full, but our hearts are often empty. Time to stop seeking the approval of others and start trusting God instead.

20: Sweet sister, call me immediately! We need to stage an intervention! You have an even lower score than this people-pleasing pro! (I was once about a 27 but when I retook the assessment just now, I'd improved to a 53. *Progress!*)

Chapter 2

What (Or Actually Who) Are We Afraid Of?

Be who you are and say what you feel, because
those who mind don't matter, and those who
matter don't mind.

—DR. SEUSS

Fear of man will prove to be a snare,
  but whoever trusts in the LORD is kept safe.

—PROVERBS 29:25

As a young teen, I loved watching the evening news with my mom. Peculiar, I know. Not a lot of my peers were more interested in Dan Rather than Dan Aykroyd, but I was. And so, as soon as I entered high school, I signed up for a journalism class. This led me to landing a spot as a reporter—and then later the sports editor—for our school's newspaper.

For the most part, I stuck to covering football games or tennis matches. Occasionally I wrote a feature article on an "athlete of the week" who'd recently made the winning three-point basket or placed first at the district gymnastics meet. But once, the editor-in-chief of the newspaper asked me to write a piece for the op-ed page. This is the editorial page where your opinion is given on a topic in an original essay.

At first, I wanted to politely decline. I was much more familiar with relaying batting averages, field goal percentages, or combined points in a swim meet. I wasn't sure I wanted to give my opinion for all the world—*I mean the school*—to see. After all, what if someone didn't agree with my opinion? What if they pushed back? Nevertheless, the editor continued to urge me on, and eventually I agreed and began my piece.

I decided to write about what I thought would be a rather noncontroversial column: a tribute to a student-athlete who had recently passed away from cancer. He was beloved by his classmates and teachers alike. He had a pleasant personality, an encouraging demeanor, and had met with some success as an athlete. I spent the next few days writing, and rewriting, until my essay was finished. It was slated to run in the next issue of our school newspaper, *The Comet's Tale*. (A clever name for our publication since our school sports teams were called the Comets.)

At first, the article was met with an overwhelmingly positive response. Classmates would stop me in the hallway to say how much they liked it. A few teachers commented to me how touching the tribute was. I was even nominated for a journalism award for outstanding editorial of the year in the network of school newspapers in my home state. I was on cloud nine. Reminiscent of Sally Field in her now-famed acceptance speech, my mind surmised, *They like me. They really like me!* But before long, my bubble was burst, sending my confidence catapulting toward the earth like a comet careening from the sky.

One afternoon, the editor-in-chief received a letter from one of the fellow seniors in the class of the now-deceased athlete. She had been a very close friend of his, and she did not hold back at all when sharing her opinion.

There was one little phrase in the editorial that she took issue with. As I was describing the impact this student-athlete had on the school, I was writing it pretty much from an angle that assumed everyone knew who he was. However, our high school had nearly two thousand students—perhaps there were some who would not be familiar with his name. And so, at the beginning of one sentence I penned a phrase that went something like this: "Perhaps you didn't even know who _____ [name of student] was, and so maybe you're thinking, 'Why does this matter to me?' It matters because a member of our Comet family is missing." I thought it was a simple way to include those in the readership who didn't know him and might not care about the article's topic. Never did I dream it would greatly anger someone. I was wrong.

The athlete's friend contended that it was disrespectful to say of a deceased person that perhaps he was a "nobody in the eyes of some of the students at the school." Of course, I never said he was a nobody. I just said that perhaps some of the readers had not heard of him. However, me calling him a nobody is how her grieving heart interpreted it.

The editor-in-chief didn't seem too concerned about the pushback from this student. After all, the letter was only signed by one person. It wasn't a petition. We didn't even get an ounce of negative feedback from anyone else. But here I am, decades later, and when I think back to that article, what I recall is not the fact that the teachers and majority of the students thought it was touching and well-written. I don't even reminisce about the nomination for the state editorial award. Nope. My brain, with laserlike focus, zeros in on the fact that a single person out of nearly two thousand did not approve.

What I'd dreaded came true. Somebody didn't like my writing. The fear of being critiqued, or even condemned, kept me from writing opinion pieces for years after that, even though seasoned journalists told me that no matter what you write, at least someone—and sometimes up to half of your readers if it was a political piece—was going to take issue with it. I wanted to be liked. All the time. And any inkling I got that someone didn't like my work was enough to edit the joy out of the craft of writing.

Years later, the same scenario would play out in different ways in my life. When I first began my speaking ministry, the event coordinators often gathered feedback from the attendees. These were compiled in an email and sent to me. I remember one particular event for which I received sixty-seven comments. Sixty-six of them were glowing and positive. However, one short sentence in the sixty-seventh one said that the attendee did not think I'd presented any new ideas in my practical workshop on home organization and that she wished she had gone to a different breakout session. Again, which of the comments velcroed to my brain? Yep. The lone critical one.

When I was a young mom, I was in charge of planning field trips for our local homeschool co-op group. At one end-of-the-year meeting—when everyone discussed which outings had been worthwhile, educational, as well as loads of fun—a half dozen people mentioned the one that I'd planned. However, when one of the moms stated that her children did not particularly care for that field trip, and she thought it should not be repeated the following year, my spirit was deflated.

I don't know where in the world I latched onto the notion that I am going to have a 100 percent batting average with all endeavors I undertake. Rather than take the not-so-lovely feed-back in stride—understanding that you can't please all the people all the time—I became emotionally allergic to doing anything that would involve a public forum of opinions. And once again, when there was negative feedback, I wrongly deduced that I had failed. To me, pleasing 99.99 percent of the people was still a big, fat fail. That .01 percent held the reins that were hitched to my emotions, capable of dragging my heart around and making my confidence fall anytime they were yanked.

The Fear Factor

At the core of my hesitancy to place my thoughts, projects, and ideas in the public forum was fear. Fear of criticism. Fear of rejection. Fear of being misunderstood. In fact, I believe that fear is so tangled up in the habit of people pleasing that it is almost impossible to define people pleasing without addressing the issue of fear. We fear hurting the feelings of others. We fear being left out. We might also be afraid of *standing* out. We may be hesitant to give our true feelings for fear of angering someone. Fear is almost omnipresent.

And here's the thing about the fear of humans. If you are tangled up in fear of what others might think of you, you can't simultaneously fear the Lord. Okay, okay. I know the phrase *the fear of the Lord* can be rather disconcerting. It was to me the first time I ever heard it. The words are often scissored out of Scripture and used in such a way that it leaves many people wondering exactly what they mean.

Some get the impression that God is out to get them; that they should be terrified of him because he is a merciless deity seeking to strike them with dreadful situations if they get even so much as one toe out of line. However, that is not at all what it means to fear the Lord. We'll explore a little bit later exactly what this term means and how—if we are truly fearing God—we can stop being so afraid of humans. But for now, let's tackle what—or rather who—you are afraid of and why.

My summer of "necessary and no" not only eradicated some tasks and responsibilities in my life, helping my stress level to go down, but it also provided me with more margin in my days to think about what had brought me to this unsettling place. I was freed to make some decisions that, going forward, would keep me from dropping a pin there again, navigating my way back to that miserable place.

I quickly realized that I didn't just like to please people, but that I was actually afraid of them. Maybe not afraid that they were going to do something to harm me physically, but afraid of what they might think of me. Or afraid of what they might say about me to others. Or afraid of looking incompetent in their eyes. Or afraid of disappointing them.

The Bible writers mince no words about this type of behavior. They call it the fear of man (in some Bible versions, "the fear of humans") and caution us that it is a snare (Proverbs 29:25). You might know the definition of the word *snare* in English. It means "a trap," much like one set to catch an animal. (Like the pesky squirrel that insists on continually finding a way to take up residence in my daughter's attic. Unfortunately, that snare isn't working well for her and the critter keeps returning!) But the word *snare*, as it is used in this portion of Scripture, carries a meaning that goes far beyond critter catching.

In Hebrew, the original language of the Old Testament, the word translated in English as *snare* is the word *moqesh*. *Moqesh* does refer to a trapping device for prey, but it also conveys the concept of bait or a lure. It indicates an animal, object, or person that is enticing, causing another animal or human to stop what they are doing and insert themselves into a dangerous situation because of the "prize" set before them. The next thing you know, they're hooked. Caught. Held captive. And it isn't a one-time catch. This alluring bait continually entices, reels in, and then drags its victim away.

Have you ever been enticed to say something you didn't really mean? You know, give your coworker an untrue compliment or rave about your neighbor's new ginormous garden statue, that you don't really care for but that you know she is obsessed with? Are you tempted to say yes to requests when you'd much rather say no just because it's easier than facing the uncomfortableness of turning the asker down? Have you been in the situation where everybody present is gushing over something you don't find oh-so remarkable, but you chime in and claim it is anyway? Is there a relationship in your life where your heartstrings are constantly tugged? You never want to upset this person because so much of their life is filled with sadness and you aren't interested in adding more disappointment. And perhaps, worst of all, is there someone with whom you have a dysfunctional relationship, and you dread ever making them upset, so you constantly take the bait and give in, just to please them?

If you answered yes to any of the above questions—or can think of another scenario where you are tempted to please someone constantly—you, my friend, have been caught in a *moqesh*. And sadly—but truthfully—in many of the instances, we don't merely fear what other people might think—or even fear we may hurt their feelings—we actually fear humans more than we fear God.

Let's flip back to the book of Galatians. Here we perceive Paul concerned about how easily his friends in this congregation were giving in to the spiritual bullying of the Judaizers. He warns them about being trapped by this people-pressure, claiming that it was

27

throwing them into confusion. At one point, he even goes so far as to inquire, "Who has bewitched you?" (Galatians 3:1). Paul was gravely concerned about how effortlessly these believers were being coerced to do and believe things that were not in accordance with God. They had elevated the opinions of humans above the ways of God.

It is interesting to prod even deeper into the words and phrases in Galatians, extracting the meaning of the original Greek words used to first write them centuries ago. To refresh your memory, here is Galatians 1:10 again:

> Am I now trying to win the approval of human beings, or of God? Or am I trying to please people? If I were still trying to please people, I would not be a servant of Christ.

The Greek word for *please* is *areskó*. At its core, it means "to agree to satisfy another in order to win their approval, affection, or attention; to meet their expectations; to willingly serve." Knowing this comprehensive definition causes the verse to pop out much more than it does when reading it in English! The caboose of this scriptural sentence tacks on a bold assertion: if the Galatians were trying to please people, they would not be a servant of Christ! We can't have it both ways when it comes to who we are trying to please. We can only serve one master.

The Greek word for *servant* in this passage is *doulos*. A doulos was indeed a servant, bound to assist a boss for a set number of years before being released from their contract. The Greek meaning of *doulos* also has another facet to it. It is that of being a person who gives themselves up fully to another's will. Ugh. Boy do I hate to admit it, but there are so many times I give myself up to someone else's will rather than boldly and bravely choosing to do what would most please God.

When faced with a choice between doing what God requires or giving in to someone else's wishes, we as followers of Jesus should choose to serve God. Now, of course, if what someone else desires is in line with God's will, that's altogether different. However, when we feel that twinge of tension—that alluring and enticing pull—we must choose to place pleasing God above placating people and determine to speak truth while trying to avoid hurting someone's feelings.

This repeating pattern of being tempted to let others call the shots rather than deciding what God would have us do isn't just a minor issue. For some, it has us in a chokehold. Sadly, it has become for us a compulsion, a craving for the approval and applause of others. How in the world did we end up hooked on this harmful human behavior? When did we become approval junkies?

How Did I Become an Approval Addict?

We don't just suddenly one day, out of the clear blue, become addicted to something. It starts small and eventually snowballs, leaving the addicted soul at the mercy of the substance, person, or behavior that now is calling all the shots.

The Merriam-Webster dictionary defines addiction as "a strong inclination to do, use, or indulge in something repeatedly."[1] Most of us are familiar with common addictions we hear of in our culture—dependence on alcohol, illegal substances, prescription painkillers, sex, and the like. But it is true that we can also become addicted to the opinions and approval of others.

Over time, we develop a strong inclination to behave in a way that gives us a warm feeling of approval—the sense that we are wanted, approved of, and that we belong. Or we make sure we don't do something to invoke an opposite response—the displeasure of someone else. Even though we may suffer from the consequences of our people-pleasing ways, we can't seem to kick the habit. And, believe it or not, there is actually a scientific aspect to our approval addiction. It centers on an element known as dopamine.

The substance known as dopamine was first discovered in 1958 by Nils-Ake Hillarp and Arvid Carlsson at the National Heart Institute of Sweden. It is a neurotransmitter that the brain manufactures whose major role is to act as a chemical messenger traversing between neurons. It is released when your brain is anticipating a reward of something pleasurable. Just the very anticipation of an enjoyable experience coming your way is enough to raise your dopamine levels. It could be a certain food, shopping, affection from a significant other, or just about anything else you enjoy—even praise and validation from others.

Here is how it works. Let's say that your favorite sweet treat is carrot cake with thick cream cheese frosting. Your brain will register this confection with pleasure. It will even increase dopamine production when you are shredding the carrots and blending up the batter in a bowl. The manufacture of dopamine will ramp up even more when you smell the cake baking in the oven. Why, your dopamine level might rise further if you smelled a carrot cake-scented oil wafting from your diffuser! When it finally comes time for you to devour your decadent dessert, the rush of dopamine acts as a reinforcement of this craving. And the pleasure you feel from this rush will compel you to ensure you're satisfied in the future with more of this delicious dish. This process and our response is a constant cycle of motivation, reward, and, finally, reinforcement.

Psychology Today says about this powerful substance:

Dopamine causes you to want, desire, seek out, and search. It increases your general level of arousal and your goal-directed behavior. Dopamine makes you curious about ideas and fuels your searching for information. Dopamine creates reward-seeking loops in the sense that people will repeat pleasurable behavior, from checking Instagram to taking drugs.[2]

So, we might think that we reflexively conduct ourselves in a way that brings approval or acclamations from others because it's simply an aggravating habit we have adopted. But in reality, something chemically is happening in our brains that strongly propels us to such repeated conduct.

Now, I don't want to give dopamine a totally bad rap. It is actually a necessary substance and something that makes us fully human. However, psychologists tell us there are natural ways to increase our dopamine level that might keep us from this pleasure-seeking loop we find ourselves caught in. Dopamine levels are raised when we exercise, get plenty of deep restful sleep, and eat foods rich in magnesium, such as whole grains, seeds, nuts, and dried beans. Also, many experts in the field of brain science say our dopamine level is increased when we spend time in prayer or meditation. The more our dopamine levels are raised by such healthy things, the less we may find ourselves seeking an increase from an addiction to a substance or positive response from others.

So how do we get off this spinning hamster wheel—chasing after approval, feeling mentally oh-so-fantastic when we temporarily find it, and then doing it all over again but failing to recognize that the short-term pleasure is actually adding to the misery in our lives?

We learn to replace the fear of humans with the fear of God. But exactly what does it mean to fear him?

In my study of this topic, I found it curious that there are two words for fear in the Bible—*charadah* and *yirah*. *Charadah* depicts a person reacting with immense anxiety or trembling with great dread. *Yirah* is defined as to respond with extreme awe and thoughtful reverence. And, yes—you guessed it. The first word is used when describing the fear of humans, but the second word is used when we talk about the fear of the Lord.

The fear of the Lord is a healthy fear. It's revering God enough to obey his commands—being in extreme awe of him and treating him with the utmost respect. There is nothing here that insinuates being scared of what he might do or shuddering and cowering at the thought of possibly ticking him off so severely that he might trigger a horrific happening aimed directly at us.

It is the fear of humans that produces anxiety in our minds, dread in our hearts, and even trembling in our bodies. Unhealthy apprehension causes us to be at the mercy of the person of whom we are frightened. But having a proper reverence and fear of God will not cause us such emotional and physical distress. It will lead us to a place of quiet confidence—even happiness—when we learn to obey his commands, even at those times when it might upset others.

Please God, Not Them

My friend and her husband were embarking on quite an adventure. They sensed God calling them to become a foster family, taking in children from difficult home situations and gifting them with a safe place to grow and thrive. They were even hoping potentially to permanently adopt a child or two, should the opportunity arise.

They'd filled out the necessary paperwork and had been approved. When I met her for coffee one afternoon, I was expecting her to gush with excitement and maybe a little apprehension.

But what I wasn't prepared for was the tale she told me through her tears.

She and her husband had told her parents what their family was about to do. She knew they would likely ask a few questions, because foster care was not something anyone in her extended family had ever done. But what she wasn't anticipating was outright discouragement. Her parents brought up every possible thing that could go wrong. They conveyed, in no uncertain terms, not only their displeasure at the decision but their lack of support. She and her husband were told to think again about their decision because these opinion-slinging relatives were certain they were about to make the wrong one.

I was heartbroken for my friend. What she and her husband were attempting was a selfless and compassionate undertaking. They were going to need all sorts of support, not only tangibly, with meals brought in and help buying items for the children, but also emotionally. How devastating for them to discover they might not be able to count on such support from this part of their extended family.

I let her talk. Then, with a hug and my words, I promised that her family could definitely count on us for help. When we finished our time together, however, her spirits were still dashed. But surprisingly, when we met later that month, her countenance and confidence had shifted. She'd acquired a calm and renewed vision about becoming foster parents. I was so curious, I just had to ask what happened.

While wrestling with her dashed emotions, she had diligently sought the Lord. After a few days of praying and reading God's Word, she'd discovered a new perspective, a conclusion she could sum up in one simple sentence. She looked at me and assuredly declared, "I finally realized that I do not need their permission to do God's will."

Wow. What a powerful pronouncement!

At first, her priorities had been misplaced. She cared more about what her parents thought of their decision than she did about what she and her husband had unmistakably discerned was God's will for this season of their life. When she stopped putting these people in the place of God, she was more willing to deal with any unpleasant outcome.

Elevating human opinions above the opinion of God was something she decided to quit doing. It wasn't easy, but she persevered. She and her husband not only became fabulous foster parents, but they ended up adopting a couple of children from within the system. And eventually—and thankfully—this set of grandparents came around, loving and treating these newly adopted children no differently than the biological grandkids. How tragic it would have been if they'd allowed her parents' initial reaction to dictate their decision instead of obeying what they felt God was calling them to do.

I've often thought about my friend's statement that day, mostly because it struck me right between the eyes when I heard her utter it. I thought about the many ways I had flip-flopped God with other people in my life, putting them in a place of authority; caring way more about what they thought about me than what I knew God was calling me to do. The kicker was—would I have the courage to stop doing it?

No Approval Necessary

At the height of the coronavirus pandemic, our twenty-two-year-old son had to suddenly return to America from Australia where he had been living on a yearlong work visa. We decided to rent him a room for a few months until he could make his next move in life, since living in the land down under had come abruptly to a halt.

We soon noticed mail addressed to him crowding our mailbox. As a member of Generation Z, he became a potential client for nearly every credit card company in existence. So many of these companies boasted a zero percent six-month introductory interest rate and no annual fee. Most also had these words stamped on the outside envelope in bright block letters: NO APPROVAL NECESSARY.

Now, if only we believers would understand this concept and live it out in our interactions with others. We do not need the approval of others. It is totally unnecessary. We have already secured the greatest approval of all, that of being a child of the Most High God.

First Corinthians 7:23 declares, "You were bought with a price; do not become bondservants of men" (ESV). We've seen this term *bondservant* surface before, the word *servant* (*doulos* in the Greek). It is someone who gives themselves up fully to another person's will. Being a people pleaser is like being a puppet, controlled by another human's will rather than submitted to the true Master, God himself.

This verse gives us a compelling reason why we should not become a bondservant of another human being. It is because we were bought with a price, referring to the ultimate price Christ paid when he gave his life as a ransom, taking our place on the cross. If we want to give an accurate depiction of the gospel to the watching world, we must live for the one who purchased our place in eternity rather than serving those around us who may pressure us, or guilt us, into doing what they wish.

However, I understand the tug at our hearts to capitulate to the desires and wishes of others—believe me, I do. Throughout my childhood and for most of my adult life I often allowed the desire to people-please decide my behavior.

We may do it because we take kindness beyond its boundaries and wrongly surmise that pleasing all the people all the time is good and godly. Or perhaps the fear of others has had such a clench on us for so many years that we keep acquiescing out of sheer habit. Or our brains may be continually craving that whopping rush of dopamine and we feel powerless to break the cycle. Whatever the reason we are caught in the whirlwind of people pleasing, at the core of it is this: *We are all tempted to devour lies when our hearts are unhappy and our souls are hungry.*

When we fail to find our satisfaction in God alone and in serving him, we can't achieve the truly contented state of mind we long for and are promised in Scripture; the blessed and happy state we read about in our Bibles. This leaves our heart hungering for more; the more only Jesus can give. Our hearts will only find true satisfaction when they find their home in him. (Which is basically a profound quote from Saint Augustine, minus the Old English lingo.)

Second Timothy 1:7 reads, "For God has not given us a spirit of timidity, but of power and love and discipline" (NASB). Let's tap into this spirit of courage, harnessing its power, truly loving people by being honest with them, and disciplining our minds to choose the fear of the Lord over the fear of others' opinions. We need not let timidity reign. We can walk upright—and with integrity—knowing that the fear of the Lord leads to wisdom and grants us knowledge.

Will you dare to become the "Decider in Chief" of your own life, making choices based on what God wants you to do rather than on what people want you to do? We must own our lives. Our lives are made up of our actions. Our actions result from our thoughts. Our thoughts are formed when we respond to others' behavior. And our responses must be in line with God's Word, carried out with confidence, not timidity.

Perhaps it's time we stopped assigning the wrong value to others, giving them power over our emotions. Of course, we are going to need to spend the rest of our lives interacting with others and navigating relationships. But we need not fear the slinging of opinions that may happen or the reactions of others when they view our choices. Oh, how I wish I could go back to my former self, at so many junctions in life, and preach this sermon to her!

To my seventeen-year-old self, I would assure her that she need not give in to the pressure to be popular by violating God's Word in order to fit in. The admiration would be temporary, but it would eat at her soul and affect her walk with Jesus.

To my twenty-two-year-old, newly married self, I would urge her to dig deep into God's Word, discovering God's directives for marriage, rather than allowing very vocal voices to bully her into adopting as doctrine all fifty-two principles "Famous Teacher So-and-So" claimed were directly taken from Scripture and God's only way of behaving as a wife.

To my twenty-seven-year-old self, I would encourage her not to walk lock-step with all the other mamas of littles from church who lived by the same parenting book—touted as the literal behavioral Bible on how to do everything from get the baby to sleep through the night to make him mind the first time he was asked; the go-to manual on breastfeeding over bottle, cloth over disposable, and homemade organic over readymade from the grocery shelves. I'd tell her if someone didn't want to be her friend just because she mothered differently, maybe it wasn't a friendship she needed at all.

To my thirty-three-year-old self, standing in the grocery store being chastised by an outspoken and combative pastor's wife—I'd tell her that just because that woman believes it's wrong to buy root beer in dark brown bottles—since it might be mistaken for actual beer—she needn't worry about causing someone to stumble into a life of alcoholism. Don't put the six-pack back. Instead, grab some vanilla ice cream and go home and treat the family to a round of root beer floats.

To my sweet self *just last week*, I'd remind her that you don't need that person's permission to do God's will. Go forward in confidence, seeking to please Christ, not the person who just weaseled their overly opinionated way into your direct messages.

To my current "tends-to-be-easily-swayed-by-people-who-appear-super-spiritual" self, I would say stop confusing another believer's advice—however seemingly prayerful and careful—with God's will. You have just as much access to the Father and to Scripture as them. They are not God. They are not *always* right. Other Christians can be helpful, but they are not fail-proof.

We must seek the Lord's approval rather than pursuing the endorsement of others. It won't always be easy, not just because we sometimes fear people more than we fear God, but because all of us have an array of personality types that make up the menagerie of people in our lives. It's time we took a look at these various people, learning how best to deal with them so they no longer hold the keys to our happiness.

I'll bet you will recognize a person or two (or three or four!) as we explore the various types of people who set themselves up as puppet master, trying to pull the strings and force us to do their will.

But don't fret. Armed with a little bit of strategy and a whole lotta Jesus's power, we can learn to cut the strings and confidently live our lives pleasing God, not them.

I'm Afraid Not

A quick online search for *fear of the Lord* will unearth at least twenty-five verses, depending on which translation of the Bible you use. Here are just a few references to the fear of the Lord—what it is, and what it does for us.

- **Proverbs 9:10:** "The fear of the LORD is the beginning of wisdom, and knowledge of the Holy One is understanding."

  In many instances, the fear of the Lord is directly tethered to the idea of wisdom and knowledge. The Hebrew word for *wisdom* in the Old Testament often referred to skill in one's work or in military battle, shrewdness in dealing with people, or prudence in dealing with religious affairs.

- **Proverbs 1:7:** "The fear of the LORD is the beginning of knowledge, but fools despise wisdom and instruction."

  This verse asserts that the fear of the Lord is the "beginning" of knowledge. What exactly is meant by beginning?

  The Hebrew definition isn't only referencing the starting point, though a starting place is certainly implied. The word *beginning* here also means "the choicest, finest, foremost," as in the first fruits of a harvest.

- **Psalm 112:1:** "Blessed are those who fear the LORD, who find great delight in his commands."

  When we fear God, Scripture calls us blessed. (And hey, who doesn't want to be blessed?) The Old Testament Hebrew term *esher* (translated *blessed* in English) simply means "how happy!" Fearing God, rather than trying relentlessly to make humans happy, will, in the end, bring delight to us if we follow his commands over the desires of others.

- **Proverbs 14:2:** "Whoever fears the LORD walks uprightly."

   To walk uprightly in this verse means "correctly, honestly, and with utmost integrity." Contrast that with people pleasing, which at times is thinly glazed with untruths as we say what we sense the other person wants to hear. When we do, our integrity might be harmed.

- **Psalm 34:11:** "Come, my children, listen to me; I will teach you the fear of the LORD."

   Did you catch it? The fear of the Lord must be learned. We may not come by it naturally, but we can be taught to do it. With a little intention, we can acquire the ability to fear the Lord.

Chapter 3

Pushers, Pouters, Guilt Bombers, and Others Who Try to Call the Shots

In trying to please all, he had pleased none.

—AESOP, *AESOP'S FABLES*

On the contrary, we speak as those approved by God to be entrusted with the gospel. We are not trying to please people but God, who tests our hearts.

—1 THESSALONIANS 2:4

I am sort of a sucker for personality tests. They fascinate me. Although I don't think it's wise to elevate them above Scripture, which teaches that Jesus can help us to overcome personality flaws and behavior patterns—I do think they can be a helpful resource for understanding why we—or those we love or work with—think, react, or behave in a certain way. And so, I have prayerfully studied them over the years, mining for nuggets of the helpful while disputing and disregarding anything unbiblical I might find.

I was first introduced to the concept of personality types in high school by a staff member at our church. She had me sharpen my #2 Ticonderoga pencil—still my pencil of choice today—and dive in. After filling in all the little dots on the pages with my answers, I found out that I was a "high I" type personality on the DISC assessment. DISC is an acronym referring to a personality test introduced by American psychologist Dr. William Marston in the late 1920s.

The *D* stands for dominance. These folks are direct and decisive problem solvers and risk takers. The *S* stands for steadiness. Such people are dependable team players who are loyal and compliant. When you meet a *C* on the DISC assessment, you will encounter someone who is a conscientious, detailed, and systematic analyzer who values quality and accuracy. The letter *I* denotes someone who is influencing. This hardwired personality type is enthusiastic—even magnetic—and greatly desires acceptance and social esteem.

Later, I would take more tests and reveal more results. On the Myers-Briggs type indicator, I am what is known as a *Consul*. The letters used to describe such persons are ESFJ—extroverted, observant, feeling, and judging. They are attentive and people-focused, and they enjoy taking part in their social community. I also more recently discovered I am a 3 wing 2 on the Enneagram, which is a combo of an achiever (3) and a helper (2) and is sometimes referred to as the Enchanter, who thrives on both getting things done and helping people out.

Well, it doesn't take someone with a psychology degree to see that someone with my particular personality likely struggles with craving the approval of others to the detriment of their own peace of mind. But people pleasers don't only come in an alphabet soup and number combo of I-E-F-S-J-3-W-2 like I do. They are givers. Perfectionists. Peacemakers. Rescuers. Helpers. Lovers. Behind-the-scenes doers. So for many reasons we may bend over backward for others, all the while knowing we are breaking our own backs in the process.

I have come to think of it in this way: many of us people-please because something in our personality, which is an obvious strength, can morph into a derailing weakness when taken to an extreme. Here are a few examples.

Perhaps you are a peacemaker. You can see all sides of a situation or argument. You long for harmony in the relationships around you, whether at work or in the home. In fact, sometimes others seek you out for your keen sense of fairness and your ability to bring calm into what otherwise might be a volatile situation. What a strength it is to have the skill set of a peacemaker! That is, until it gets taken to an extreme and gets all out of whack. Because peacemakers crave peace, they don't like to rock the boat. Or stir the pot. Or make any noise while walking on the eggshells scattered before them. Therefore, they might have the tendency to not speak up and speak their mind. They often give in just to get along. Their go-with-the-flow personality sometimes finds them being swept out to sea by the riptide caused by the strong personality of an individual who they are afraid to upset.

Or take the giver. What a generous and others-centered personality these dear souls have. They go the extra mile. They're often extravagantly generous behind the scenes. They care about the welfare and needs of others so deeply. It is always at the forefront of their mind. However, sometimes the giver gets squeezed too tight, wringing every ounce of heart and soul right out of them. When their generous personality is not kept in check by physical and emotional limitations, they can easily cross a line. They may become emotionally depleted, giving and serving beyond what is needful, or even healthy. And then, if they feel overly sorry for themselves, they can begin to feel like a martyr.

With so many fabulous characteristics, there is usually a flip side. When taken to an extreme, people can transmute a strength into a weakness—a weakness that often leaves them craving the acceptance and approval of others despite what it might actually do to them. Learning to deal with our unique personalities and the pitfalls that lie in our lives due to how we are made is an important concept to explore.

But here's the thing. Yes, many of us people-please due to our personality makeup. However, sometimes the "disease to please" rears its annoying head because we get to a place where we allow others to fill a role in our lives they were never meant to occupy.

In his excellent book *When People Are Big and God Is Small*, author Edward Welch introduces the fascinating concept of how we give people in our lives various "shapes." He writes,

> Notice some of the common shapes we give others:
> - *People are gas pumps that fill us.*
> - *People are sought-after tickets to acceptance and fame.*
> - *People are priests who have the power to make us feel clean and okay.*
> - *People are terrorists, we never know when they will strike next.*
> - *People are dictators whose every word is law. They are in complete control."*[1]

I've observed myself allowing someone at some time to play every single one of those shapes in my life.

Let's explore now not only the shapes others take in our lives, but the personalities they possess—all those people wanting us to leap through the hoop they're currently holding, landing on the other side in the exact spot they've chosen for us.

And so . . . Givers, Peacemakers, Enchanters, Helpers, and other overly accommodating folks, are you ready? Meet the Pushers, Pouters, Guilt Bombers, and other people who try to call the shots.

Up first, we encounter the Pusher.

Why So Pushy?

When I was first married, cell phones were still dumb—as in not yet "smart phones" with internet and search engines available at the touch of a finger. One rare, quiet fall afternoon, a friend of mine—who had a rather dominant and abrasive personality and whose bad side I never wanted to get on—gave me a ring. She wanted to know what company we'd recently hired to clean our carpets. Because I couldn't text her a link like I can today, I did what I thought would help. I heartily recommended the name of the business, a local company that had done a fabulous job. That done, I hoped to get back to my afternoon of quiet before starting supper for the family. But that was not the way she wanted to end the call. What I thought was a simple phone call with an easy answer took a turn straight toward the old push-and-pull of appeasement. It all began when she asked a seemingly innocent follow-up question: "Do you happen to have their phone number handy?"

I answered her question, stating that no, I didn't. Then— trying to ward off the request I was sure was careening my way—I added that she could easily look it up in the phone book. She sighed a little and, in my mind, I thought, *Here it comes!* And then, like countless times in the past, this pusher friend of mine began . . . well . . . *pushing*!

With a touch of frustration in her voice, she declared that she was upstairs in her bedroom and her phone book was all the way down on the lower level of the house in a drawer in the kitchen.

Looking up the phone number herself would require her to get up from what she was doing and scurry down a flight of stairs and then back up again on what she said was a "crazy-busy day." And so, she confidently announced the remedy to her pressing I-need-that-phone-number dilemma. You guessed it. She assertively declared, in a way that *kinda* seemed like a suggestion (but not really, since her voice had suddenly taken on a slightly irritated tone), "Can't *you* just look it up for me?"

Well, I certainly could. No law against that in my country, state, county, township, or even my neighborhood's HOA. However, I myself was nowhere near a phone book either. I was in our finished basement—enjoying some rare alone time, reading a book before heading back into my own crazy-busy life. For me to look it up would also require some staircase travel—thank you very much—as I'd need to go upstairs to grab our phone directory from the kitchen drawer. I'd like to say I held firm and told her she'd have to find the number herself since I didn't have time to run and get it for her, which was true. However, due to her strong "pusher" personality—and my strong dislike of any tension or conflict—I stopped what I was doing and trekked upstairs.

After giving her the phone number and hanging up the phone, I was infuriated. Naturally, I didn't let her in on that little fact. What I didn't realize back then was that it was *myself* I should have been mad at, not my forceful friend.

Those in our life who behave this way are pushers. Strong. Assertive. Controlling. Sometimes even slightly caustic or outright combative; able to utilize their words and facial expressions in a way that brings results. They sabotage you with their *shoulds*—both spoken and implied, telling you what you should do and also when you should do it.

We do their bidding because we aren't brave enough to stand

up to their dominant personality. Especially if we are more of a subtle soul with a quiet demeanor. Pushers get what they want because they are proficient at intimidating and aren't afraid to bully others if needed.

Yes, pushers push. We cave. And we please and appease to get out of their way, which results in them also getting their way. Again and again.

Why the Long Face?

Next, we have the Pouters. Pouters are powerful. They don't force you to behave a certain way through their domineering demeanor. They play to your sympathies, reeling you in because you feel sorry for them. Their melancholy manner is highly effective. It gets them the results they want and leaves you sipping a swirling cocktail of emotions—a bit of sweet satisfaction because you helped out a needy soul stirred together with a splash of bitterness over being manipulated by their gloomy disposition.

There was a period of time in my not-too-distant past when I was constantly manipulated by a professional pouter. Maybe you know the type. It's your great Aunt Agatha who drops her smile when the extended family is planning for the upcoming holiday season and it appears the majority don't want to have family Christmas at her house for the third year in a row. You pick up on her despondency over this decision. You can see it in her eyes. Her slouched shoulders also give a clue. "Is that okay with you, Auntie Agatha, or were you hoping we'd all hang out at your place again this year?" you inquire.

"Oh no. It's fine. You all just do whatever you want," she says with a sigh. "It really doesn't matter to me. I'm just getting up there in years and don't know how many more Christmases I'll be around to host the get-together."

So, her words say she is fine and that y'all can do what you want. Meanwhile, her body language, facial expressions, and choice of words are *screaming* that it really does matter to her *a lot* and you have just crushed her Christmas dreams like you crush candy canes with a wooden mallet for your homemade holiday peppermint bark each year.

Aunt Agatha is able to tug at the heartstrings of the decision makers in the bunch. They get sucked into her swirl of sadness and capitulate. They decide the shindig will be at her place. Maybe it's easier to just let her get her way than to deal with the fallout of her fallen countenance and any potential future manipulating behavior. Such behavior might include more comments to garner sympathy or even private one-on-one conversations with key players, which may only add to the drama and make everyone miserable. Just let her get her way. After all, she usually does, so why stop now?

Pouters know how to play to our emotions. And this practice often gets them their way. But is that always the best thing for a pouter? Is continuing to let them play this game helping their relationships be beneficial, godly, and productive? Or is it contributing to their repeated sad scenarios, which paint them in a negative light and bring dysfunction to the relationships they do have?

While we might think we are alleviating sadness when we give in to a pouter, we are only heaping on trouble upon trouble. Trouble for us—and also trouble for them.

Get 'Em with Guilt

Pushers. Pouters. And next, we have the Guilt Bombers. Oh boy. Stand back if you have one of those in your circle of friends, the cubicle next to you at work, or—worst of all—your family. You might get hit with an awful "Incoming!" if you don't duck fast.

Guilt bombers don't control through their dominance in a bossy "my way or the highway" manner. They don't turn their smiles into frowns, garnering sympathy and making it all about their happiness. These cunning folks lob a grenade of guilt our way, making us feel as if we owe them something or stealthily suggesting that we aren't pulling our own weight.

This might be the friend with whom you occasionally grab coffee but who never, ever offers to pay. After all, she has made offhanded comments about her limited income and the fact that it "must be nice" to have a secure job with benefits since she lives from contract to contract with her residential painting company. You feel guilt-ridden when you are out together and so you always pick up the tab.

Or how about the relative who seems to be able to annually slip in a sob story when it comes time to plan the group gift for grandma for her birthday? Things are always going wrong for her and she is stressed out from working so many overtime hours. She has implied a time or two—both through words and actions— that you probably have more time on your hands since you are a part-time, work-from-home mom who puts in half days rather than full ones like she does.

Or how about this: You've recently gotten to know another parent who has a daughter on the same softball team as your middle schooler. After discovering that you live just a half mile apart in developments next door to each other, you begin to share rides. Things are bumping along quite nicely with this strategy, which saves both of you gas and it also frees up a little time each week for you to spend doing something other than carting sweaty adolescents around.

However, the wheels begin to fall off the old SUV as you notice that the other mom starts offering legit-sounding excuses as to why she can't run the carpool that day. And they aren't just believable; they are also ones that make you feel a bit sorry for her and therefore guilty about asking her to take her fair share of turns. Her mom is sick and needs to be taken to the doctor's office. She has a splitting migraine headache and needs to lie down in a dark room for a while. Direct deposit hasn't reached her bank yet, so she doesn't have the funds to put gas in the tank until tomorrow. Her dysfunctional and critical sister-in-law—of whom she is greatly intimidated—just texted and wants to stop over in a few hours, so she needs to clean her house—and fast! To be nice and accommodating, you grab the girls and run them home.

With each of these situations, your sense of guilt has been triggered. Perhaps you are afraid of looking insensitive to their life or financial situation. And then, *boom!* another guilt bomb goes off, you outwardly smile and take on the task, stacking more on your already too-full plate.

This is not to say there aren't indeed legitimate times when someone comes up against an unfortunate situation and you should go the extra mile to help them. (More about legit times to please others in the sidebar at the end of the chapter.) But learn to look for patterns. If you see things go awry that tempt you to feel a bit guilty and prompt you to roll up your sleeves to remedy the situation, beware. Also beware of those who repeatedly try to play on your sympathy by pointing out their lack of funds, resources, or even opportunities, in order to guilt-bomb you into action. Prayerfully and carefully proceed when you are dealing with these shame-inducing souls. There is a difference between feeling convicted by God to take action and being guilt-bombed and shamed by someone. Shut the door on shame!

Me First!

We aren't finished yet. There is another type of shot-callers. These are what I call the "Me-First Maximizers." They are not outright narcissists. They don't take it quite that far. (And if you are dealing with a truly narcissistic person, I suggest you seek professional help or check out a great resource for this trying situation listed in the resource section.)

In a way, I gotta hand it to the me-first maximizers. They are crafty. Creative. Cunning. And they know exactly how to work a situation to their advantage, making sure they come out on top. Of course, they are able to pull this all off with a pleasant disposition, so you might not even notice it is happening.

I had a several years' stretch years ago of being closely connected to a me-first maximizer. As in working side-by-side on some projects that brought both of us income. While many aspects of this person's personality were wonderful—hardworking, detail-oriented, willing to come up with plans of attack, punctual, and pleasant—there was one consistent characteristic that caused me a lot of grief, sparked resentment in my heart, and which I allowed to make me so angry sometimes that I could hardly see straight. However, like a good keep-'em-happy soldier, I never let my frustration show.

What was this habit of character? Whenever a situation presented itself where one person would get the advantage, get the lighter workload, or earn the most money—basically any situation where there was a winner and a loser—this person always came out the winner. Always! No matter how many times only two pieces of pie were left in the proverbial pan, they always snatched the biggest piece, leaving me with the teenier one.

The projects we worked on typically included both really enjoyable tasks as well as not-so-pleasant ones. Let's say 75 percent of the duties involved creativity—invigorating and pleasant to do. The other 25 percent was grunt work—lots of boring and very little that was enjoyable.

This person would take initiative, jump in, and happily draw up a work plan. Now, they seemed to be doing it in a very conscientious way, carefully dividing up the total work of the project 50/50. However, the 50 percent I was assigned consisted of most of the not-so-fun stuff. None of that was assigned to them. So, I was responsible for half of the work of the total project, alright. That seemed entirely fair on the surface. Only they'd conveniently made sure their 50 percent was composed of all "yay!" and mine was only part "yay!" and the rest total "yuck."

They maximized situations to put themselves first in other instances as well. Many phone calls were involved in the projects we were doing. And this was back before the days of unlimited, free long-distance on a cell phone. One year I racked up an over $900 long-distance phone bill. I carefully highlighted all the calls I made, and then presented this person with the total just after the first of the year when I was gathering all my receipts and papers for my taxes. I thought, to be equitable, we should split the cost evenly. End of story. Fair enough, right?

Nope. Not with a me-first maximizer around.

They pointed out to me the fact that making phone calls was on *my* side of the task list ledger and that they'd diligently done their assigned work. "Besides," they added, "You can always write it off on your taxes." Huh? Writing it off on my taxes, when I was in a 25 percent tax bracket still meant I was out nearly $700 for something that had benefited us both equally.

But perhaps their most maximizing moment came the day they swung by my house to drop off something. I answered the door surrounded by my three young children, who I was desperately trying to wrangle down for a nap. I had just packaged up a half dozen orders of one of our products that needed to be mailed to customers. I asked them if they minded dropping off the envelopes at the post office on their way back home. It was a simple ask. An easy task. If they did it, I wouldn't need to get my children up from their naps by 4:30 in order to buckle them in their car seats and hightail it down to the post office before the last round of mail left at five.

Besides, I knew this person was headed to a store near the post office. So, I asked if they could do that for me—well, actually for *us* because the envelopes held our mutual products. I was not at all prepared for the answer they gave.

"No," they began. "That's not going to work. I need to get home to get a jump start on dinner. Can't you just do it later today?"

I was flabbergasted. Swinging by the post office and placing these packages in the drop box would not even require them to get out of their car! It did mean they would need to drive three whole blocks out of their way. Three blocks! But they stuck to their guns, and I didn't push back. Once again, they had maximized a situation to put themselves first.

Now here's the thing about a me-first maximizer; a sure way to tell if someone has this characteristic or not. Ask yourself this: If you turned the tables, placing them in your position and plopping yourself in their spot, would the situation go down oh-so differently? If the answer is yes, you've got a bonafide, me-first maximizer on your hands.

I know this person would never have agreed to foot a whole $900 bill for the phone calls that needed to be made for the business. They would have claimed that it wasn't fair. If I had split up the task list in a way that had given them all the unpleasant work, they would have protested. And, they would have sweetly—but pointedly—called me out for being selfish if I refused to drive three blocks out of my way to run an errand that would have saved them from carting all their young children out on a snowy, winter day.

My mom has a phrase that sums up such a person quite accurately: "They just can't see past the end of their own nose!" Yep. That's it. Their myopic ways allow them to only see situations from their vantage point and then decide accordingly, making sure they come out on top.

Rip the Bandage

I finally came to a point where I had to do something about the calculating person to whom I was constantly capitulating. My treatment in this relationship was not only starting to affect my mental health and sleep patterns, but it was also causing anger and resentment to well up inside my heart, leading to an ugly place that was affecting my walk with the Lord. Like the times my mom would have to rip the bandage off my skinned knee, I realized I needed to do something quick that might be painful. However, it would lead me to a place of healing and peace.

In my situation, it was my decision to sever ties with my "me-first maximizer" partner. I'd love to say I did this in a brave and bold way, standing up for myself. However, that would not be the truth. My knees were knocking, my voice was shaking, and I felt like I might lose my lunch. But one day, over a decade ago, I decided that the pain would be worth it and so I did it. And am I ever thankful I did!

I had an idea for a new product, one that was right up my alley and related to something I was known for. When this person got wind of my idea, they inserted themselves right into the conversation, speaking as if they were already part of the project. I mustered all my gumption and then sweetly, but straightforwardly announced, "Actually, I think I'm going to do this one alone." That was it. It wasn't as strong as it should have been. I probably shouldn't have said, "I *think* I'm going do this one alone." I should have just stated, "I'm going to do this one alone." But hey, I was an absolute newbie at this gig.

And then, at long last . . . *I was free*! I was able to work, plan, and dream about the projects and endeavors God was calling me to pursue. I no longer felt compelled to follow someone else's plan for me.

Are you ready to deal with the shot-callers in your life, the ones who get you to do what they want you to do without you ever even putting up a fuss? It will sting for a minute as you rip that capitulating behavior out of your repertoire of responses. However, being controlled by others and their pushy, pouty, guilt-giving, or self-serving way is not honoring to God. You are living your life according to their will, not his. My friends, this is not a healthy way to live. It will drain your mental energy, spark anger and resentment in your heart, and keep you from living confidently in your call to display the gospel to others in your various relationships.

Take some time to identify any people in your life who fall into one of these categories. Begin now to pray that God will empower you to break the negative pattern of behavior you have been gripped by that has opened the door to their repeatedly bad behavior. Then, get ready. You are about to do something you should have done long, long ago.

Be honest with them.

Yes, your knees may knock. Your voice may shake. Your stomach may be filled with fluttering butterflies that rival the latest nature-inspired pic on Instagram. But you can do it. I know you can! And oh, what freedom you will experience when you do.

It's time we start making straightforward—but loving—truth-telling our greatest go-to tool.

Exceptions to the Rule

Is there ever a time when it is right to please others? Yes, of course! However, that time is not all the time. That's where many of us people pleasers go wrong.

Theologian Charles Haddon Spurgeon once professed, "Discernment is not knowing the difference between right and wrong. It is knowing the difference between right and almost right."[2] Such discernment is needed in matters of pleasing others. We need to not go overboard in either direction, asserting that we are never to behave as someone else wishes or, the opposite, that we are always to do so.

Although the bulk of this book is dedicated to helping you stop over-pleasing others, trapped in a prison because of your constant capitulation, let's look at some of the times we are urged in Scripture to place another's wishes above our own.

- *Children are to seek to please and obey their parents* (Ephesians 6:1–3; Colossians 3:20).
- *We are instructed to please those in authority over us in work situations* (Ephesians 6:5–8).
- *Spouses are encouraged to think of each other's desires and wishes* (Ephesians 5:15–33).
- *We are told to not only think of our own interests, but also to the interests of others* (Philippians 2:3–5).
- *We are to honor and obey those God has placed in positions of authority in our government, knowing they were placed there by him* (Romans 13:1–7).

- *We are to be devoted to one another in love, honoring others above ourselves* (Romans 12:10).
- *We are to please our neighbors, for their good, in order to build them up* (Romans 15:2).
- *We seek to "become all things to all people" in order to win them to the gospel* (1 Corinthians 9:19–23).

So, what is this fine line between right and almost right when it comes to people pleasing? Well, it is one thing to constantly feel the pull of pleasing others, regardless of what they are asking you to do. However, if in the overarching umbrella of seeking to please God, you end up pleasing people, that is a different thing entirely. Seeking to live a life that glorifies God will end up pleasing others in the process. The trouble comes in when we only seek to fulfill *their* wishes, regardless of whether it fits into God's overarching plan. Others being pleased with our behavior is a by-product of our seeking to glorify God. It is not the main objective.

Chapter 4

Well, to Be Honest with You

Honesty saves everyone's time.
—ANONYMOUS

*And stop lying to each other. You have given up
your old way of life with its habits.*
—COLOSSIANS 3:9 CEV

Most Sunday mornings, I love going to church. It gives me a chance to get out of my normal work-from-home mom uniform, which usually consists of a graphic tee shirt and comfy jeans paired with my favorite baby blue cable-knit slippers. I even love the venue. It's in a revitalized, eclectic part of town with lots of original brick and new graffiti-like artwork on the coffee houses and vintage resale shops in Michigan's REO Town—named for Ransom Eli Olds, a pioneer in the local auto industry. When I was a child, the building where I now worship every Sunday was a bowling alley. Later it sported a nightclub. Most recently it housed a discount furniture store until our church set up shop there as one of its venues.

About 9:55 each week, I walk in and tuck my Bible under my arm so I can grab a cup of hazelnut coffee and find my seat with my husband, usually near our son and his wife. I grow from the sermons. I love the assortment of music. (Our church has over ten different bands that range in style from acoustic guitar to 80s pop to hip-hop. One even boasts a spoken word poet.) Most of all, I'm grateful we have people from diverse ethnicities and walks of life ranging in age from infants, Gen Zers sporting tattoos and man buns, and senior saints with gray hair and glasses.

However, one Sunday morning found me wanting to ditch my coffee and break free from that place, running as far as my middle-aged legs would take me. What on earth caused me to want to escape the place I adore so much? It was when the teaching pastor that day made an assertion smack dab in the middle of a sermon I was rather enjoying, completely wrecking it—and me. It was this: *People pleasers often lie.*

Suddenly no longer was I a face in a crowd of hundreds, sweetly sipping my creamy hot beverage and taking color-coded notes in the open Bible on my lap. I felt as if one of the spotlights that hung from the ceiling—normally fixated on the stage—had suddenly drop-swiveled directly toward me, placing my bright red face in portrait mode. I felt exposed. I imagined everyone giving me the side-glance knowing surely that the pastor was referring to me. The jig was up.

I fought my urge to run away. However, I did toy with the idea of getting up to pretend to use the bathroom. Nevertheless, I stayed seated until the pointed and painful message was over. I even managed to mutter a few words to Pastor Justin about how his sermon really convicted me. And it did. It wasn't one of those times when you nod in agreement, sensing a slight prick in your heart, but mosey on your way and never adjust your behavior because of it. I've done that more times than I'd like to admit. No, that stunning sentence, which pricked my heart at the start of my summer of necessary and no, was a catalyst to me finally breaking out of the prison of people pleasing. Oh, I knew I pleased others because I wanted to appear nice. I even admitted fear played a part in it. But that morning, I had to concede that my pastor was right. People pleasers often lie. And I was a fantastic fibber.

Deception in the life of a people pleaser gets cleverly cloaked as concern and care. After all, we're only shading the truth ever-so-slightly in order to not hurt someone's feelings, right? Or maybe we're afraid they can't handle the truth and we don't want to cause them mental distress. Or, if we were totally forthright with them, our truthful words would cause them sadness or maybe even anger. We're only twisting the truth a teeny bit and we are doing it for them, not for us. But are we?

When we thinly glaze our phrases with untruth—let's say when answering someone who has asked us to give them our opinion about their outfit—are we really doing it for their benefit? If the outfit is not flattering, is it in their best interest that we fail to be forthright and instead say, "Looks great!"? Isn't it really for our own benefit? We don't want awkwardness to be hanging in the air. Of course, we can always say a fashion choice just isn't our style but suits *them* well, if indeed it does. But we must ask ourselves if we fear a slight fracture in our friendship if we don't say what they are hoping to hear. In reality, often our little white lies are all about little ol' us.

Lying in order to please or appease someone is not a new phenomenon. It has been going on forever. In fact, some of our biblical brothers and sisters were doing it centuries and centuries ago. Let's take a look at a few of their stories now.

You Can't Hide Your Lyin' Eyes

When it comes to lies, it almost appears as if there are categories of untruth. As I already mentioned, someone might tell what is classified as a fib. It's seemingly harmless. It's easily gotten away with.

Then we have justified falsehoods. These lies are done for a greater good, such as when, during World War II, someone who was hiding the Jews from the Nazis might lie when asked outright if they were doing so. They did it in order to preserve someone's life. It was done for the greater good and therefore totally justified.

And let's not forget the lies of convenience, told so as to ward off any ensuing drama or maybe ensuing work. Then there are lies of vanity, meant to bolster our egos and make ourselves look better. And finally, we have the whoppers. These lies are real doozies, such as lying on your taxes or to the police when asked if you know something about a crime. These seem to be the most serious of all.

However, one category of lies seems to be the easiest to tell. At least I have found this to be the case in my life. We find a prime example of such a lie when we look at our biblical brother and sister Abraham and Sarah.

Abraham was a crucial Old Testament character. In fact, he is very important in the history not only of Christianity but also of Judaism and Islam. God told Abraham, first called Abram, that he would be the father of many nations (Genesis 15:5; 22:17). When that promise didn't take place in the timeline Abraham had hoped for, he took matters into his own hands. His wife Sarah, known as Sarai at the time, was childless; instead of waiting for the Mrs. to become a mama, he slept with her handmaid Hagar in order to conceive a child, a culturally popular practice at that time.

Later, however, Sarah and Abraham *did* produce a child in

their advanced years whose name was Isaac. But that is not the part of the story we're going to examine. Let's rewind the timeline back a bit, before the birth of Abe's two bouncing baby boys. We pick up the story in Genesis 12.

Sarah and Abraham came upon some difficult times. Due to a severe famine that struck their homeland of Canaan, they were forced to go down to Egypt and live as foreigners. As they were approaching the border, Abraham grew concerned about a possible situation that might arise in this new land.

Scripture states that his wife was a total babe (my loose translation). He was afraid that when the Egyptians saw her—and then discovered she was his wife—they would kill him in order to have her. And so, he came up with a plan. "Say you are my sister, so that I will be treated well for your sake and my life will be spared because of you" (Genesis 12:13). And sure enough, Sarah's striking beauty did not go unnoticed in Egypt. She was taken into Pharaoh's palace. However, the Lord caused terrible plagues to pile up on Pharaoh and his household because of this. When Abraham was summoned and questioned, Pharaoh ordered them out of the country.

Now you think old Abe would have learned his lesson, but this was not the case. He repeats the falsehood all over again. While moving from region to region, the couple landed in a place known as Gerar. Abraham—once again afraid that he may lose his life because a high official might want his wife for his own—didn't introduce Sarah to the residing royalty, King Abimelek, as "The little Mrs." He declared, "She is my sister" (Genesis 20:2).

This time, God came in a dream to King Abimelek, who had taken quite a shining to Sarah. He revealed to the king that she was a married woman. Luckily, he had been practicing social distancing. (Okay, okay, another slight paraphrase!) According to Genesis 20:4, he "had not gone near her."

Very early the next morning, the king summoned Abraham wanting to know why in the world he had lied. Abraham came clean and confessed that he'd been deceptive because he feared for his life. And then he added, "Besides, she really is my sister, the daughter of my father though not of my mother; and she became my wife. And when God had me wander from my father's household, I said to her, 'This is how you can show your love to me: Everywhere we go, say of me, "He is my brother"'" (Genesis 20:12–13).

Okay, at first blush it might appear that this lie falls in the "whopper" category. She was his spouse, not his sister. He was making up this lie out of the thin, blue air. But his lie was not a whopper. It falls into a different category. It was the kind many of us tell today. It wasn't an outright lie. It was actually a half-truth. And when pressed about it by Abimelek, he attempted to highlight the half-correct part and minimize the half-bologna portion. However—as I often lectured my dear offspring when they were kids—a half-truth is still a whole lie.

Now, you will find different Bible scholars who will explain this whole sister-wife scenario that seems much more 2020s reality show than ancient Bible account. Some say they were indeed half-siblings. In Genesis 20:12, we see Abraham's reasoning, "Besides, she really is my sister, *the daughter of my father though not of my mother*; and she became my wife" (emphasis mine).

Still other theologians say that a deeper dive into Abraham's ancestry implies that Sarah was actually his niece through his brother Haran. Whatever the case, Abraham's half-truth was meant to deceive the royalty with whom he was interacting, denying that he was her spouse and making them think otherwise.

What do half-truths look like in our lives today? And more importantly, why do we tell these fabrications rather than come clean and tell the truth, the whole truth, and nothing but the truth? I'll stick my neck out and confess a half-truth I told recently. I'm not proud of it, however clever it may be. No matter how much creativity goes into concocting my half-truths, they are still wrong!

There came a knock on my door. I peered out and saw a mom with her two darling young daughters. Their sweet faces glowed with anticipation as well as a little nervousness. They were selling Girl Scout cookies. Instantly, my thoughts started to do a back-and-forth dance. I wanted to encourage the girls in their business endeavor, surmising that they might be apprehensive and anxious at trying to close the deal on a box or two of Thin Mints or Samoas. But on the other hand, I didn't want any Girl Scout cookies. I was trying to watch my sugar intake, and I knew having those delicious treats in my house was going to be a major temptation.

I opened the door and greeted them. They gave me their little spiel and then looked up to see what my reply would be. "Oh, I'm sorry," I began. "I have nieces who are big into Girl Scouts and I always buy my cookies from them. But good luck in the neighborhood. Hope you sell a ton of boxes." They thanked me for my time and went on their way.

I closed the door and went back to my cup of pour-over coffee at the kitchen table feeling like a jerk. Just like old Abe, I'd told a half-truth. Or at least I implied a truth that was not so. Yes, I have nieces who have donned Girl Scout uniforms. However, I didn't buy any cookies from them this year, even if I made it sound as if I did. In fact, it's been quite a few years since they were Girl Scout age. But notice my cunningness. I didn't say that they *were* Girl Scouts, just that they "were big into Girl Scouts" and I always bought my cookies from them. It's true. If I ever did purchase a pack or two, it was from them. It just had been a while. (Wink, wink.)

Looking back, I should have been truthful and told them that we were trying to stay away from sweets. I could have wished them well in their endeavor and made a $10 donation to their Girl Scout cookie fund. In fact, I've promised myself this is exactly what I'm going to do the next time those beanie-wearing cherubs show up on my front porch.

Another form our lies may take is when they are told as flattery. Flattery, also known as false adulation or blandishment, is excessive or insincere praise. It is usually told to make the other person feel better about themselves but also to help advance the interests of the one doing the flattering. While gossip can be defined as saying something behind someone's back that you'd never say to their face, flattery is much the reverse. It is uttering words to someone's face that you'd never say behind their back because they are totally untrue.

When we flatter, we lie. The pages of Scripture are chock-full of warnings against this seemingly effective tool—but a tool that often backfires.

Read these words found in Psalm 12:2. I have written them here in the Amplified version of the Bible, a version that seeks to accurately depict the original Hebrew or Greek language in which the verse was penned. It reads:

> They speak deceitful and worthless words to one another;
> With flattering lips and a double heart they speak.

The word rendered *flattering* in the original Hebrew is the word *chelqah*, meaning "smooth, slippery, and agreeable." It is also used in many places to mean a portion of ground or the ground one is presently standing on. Combine these together and the picture becomes clear. We are surely standing on a slippery slope when we choose to flatter with our lips.

The other part of this verse that intrigues me is the notion of a double heart. The concept conveyed here is that someone who is flattering with their lips really has two hearts—one that is true to their inner soul and one that is portrayed to the person hearing the lies. This second heart is insincere and even downright deceptive.

Elsewhere in Scripture, we see what flattering can do to us. We usually only have in mind what it can do *for* us; the immediate results we seek when we falsely inflate the ego of another person. But what about what it is doing *to* us? Let's not fool ourselves thinking that we can come out of a flattering situation unharmed. We often can't. Flattery has results and they aren't very pretty.

Proverbs 26:28 lays out one of the consequences:

> A lying tongue hates those it hurts,
>   and a flattering mouth works ruin.

The Hebrew word for *ruin* in this verse is *midcheh.* Interestingly, it is the only occurrence of this word in the entire Bible. It means "a method for, or occasion of, stumbling." When we work our flattery, we are in for a fall.

A few chapters later in Proverbs, the book of wisdom, the topic of flattery bubbles to the surface again, offering a depiction we discussed earlier.

> Those who flatter their neighbors
>   are spreading nets for their feet. (Proverbs 29:5)

Flattery is an attempt to trap, entangle, or snare someone by our feigned kindness or admiration. When we flatter, we are attempting to catch them garnering their adulation. Instead, we just might get ourselves in a tangled mess by our lies.

Before we leave the book of Proverbs, check out one more verse about the deceptive practice of flattering someone.

> Whoever rebukes a person will in the end gain favor
> rather than one who has a flattering tongue.
> (Proverbs 28:23)

Notice something about this statement: it's calling us to do a rather unpleasant thing. Who likes to rebuke someone? And who in the world enjoys being rebuked themselves? But there is a promise tucked into the verse that will be fulfilled when we are truly honest. We are told that we will gain favor. Isn't that the thing we are often searching for in the first place when we flatter? We think our flattery will gain us favor, but often it just traps us or backfires.

The word *favor* here means "acceptance and grace." But take a peek at *when* we are told this acceptance and grace might flow our way. It's not at the moment we are truthfully pointing out something that might be unpleasant. It states that we will find favor "in the end." This phrase in the original language means "afterward, at a future date." The person to whom we are speaking the truth might not throw their arms around us with gratefulness the moment we speak it. But later—in the future once they've had time to think about it—they will be more grateful to us than if we'd lied with flattering lips.

The old cliche is true: flattery gets us nowhere. But flapping our flattering lips isn't the only time we lie. We also avoid the truth at times, hoping it may also enable us to avoid a fight.

Avoiding the Battle Cry (Which Makes You Want to Cry!)

I stood in the hallway near the kitchen listening to my husband chat with a few extended family members whose home we were visiting. I feigned interest in the new calendar that hug on the wall, flipping through it as if to admire its stunning nature photos. In reality, I could hear a conflict beginning to arise and saw the look on my husband's face that indicated, "Get me outta here!"

I was having the exact thought myself, while also praying I wouldn't get pulled into the heated discussion. No such luck. Soon I heard the words, "Well, Karen, what do you think? You certainly can't agree with your husband!"

I could feel my face beginning to flush. I knew I was doomed. I did agree with my husband on the important-to-me political issue that was being hashed over. But I knew that telling the truth was going to intensify the conflict even more, ruining the summer picnic we were just about to enjoy in the backyard.

My sweet husband came to my rescue, piping up and redirecting the conversation on a dime. I breathed a sigh of relief, grateful I hadn't been pulled into the back-and-forth banter with my combative kin but could enjoy my potato salad in peace.

You've been there, right? Leary to speak honestly, knowing it might bring about conflict? The battle cry suddenly sounds, making you want to cry your eyes out.

This subject is a little more tender, and I know for some of you it may bring about unpleasant memories. I know it does for me. In my past there was a person who had a tendency to be abusive, usually when they were under the influence of alcohol. I learned early on in my dealings with this person that—especially if they were even slightly inebriated—that I could save myself from the heat of battle by not speaking truthfully which—if I did—would only set into motion a stint of conflict with them. (Again, let me emphatically say that if you are dealing with a truly abusive person, please reach out to the National Abuse Hotline through the information in the footnote in chapter one.)

It's true that honesty might infuse a little tension into the air or even create colossal conflict in our conversation. So, we shade the truth a bit in order to avoid such unpleasant interactions. We instantly try to go all Switzerland and play the neutral, peace-loving role. But are we attempting to actually *make* peace or just to *keep* peace, maintaining the status quo without any ruffled feathers, simmering emotions, or flaring tempers.

Ronald Reagan once said, "Peace is not absence of conflict, it is the ability to handle conflict by peaceful means."[1] We can learn to be people who handle conflict—or even potential conflict—by peaceful means, with a calm but candid tone. And we can find some advice for doing so in the book of Proverbs. Glance carefully over these words from Proverbs 15:1, taken from the Amplified Bible.

> A soft and gentle and thoughtful answer turns away wrath,
> But harsh and painful and careless words stir up anger.

Most of us in the people pleasing department don't typically spout off words that are harsh and painful. (Or maybe you are like me and you only tend to do that with your immediate family, who *has* to love you.) Instead, I want to turn our attention to a few other adjectives we see in this verse, specifically the words *thoughtful* and *careful*.

Do your words sometimes just tumble off your tongue without you giving vigilant thought to what you're saying? Especially when we are trying to defuse conflict before it even starts, we sometimes panic. We say things we really don't mean all in an effort to keep things at an even keel. What if instead, we prayerfully, thoughtfully, and carefully choose our words, being totally truthful but in a way that shows our sincerity and does not lead to conflict. Let me give you a fictional example.

Your sister-in-law—with whom you have a repeating conflict when it comes to who is going to be in charge of planning the extended family holiday gathering—calls to discuss this year's Thanksgiving celebration. You're fairly certain she does not want to host it, even though her house is large enough and there's nothing out of the ordinary going on in her life. You, on the other hand, are not really chomping at the bit to offer your home as the meeting place this year either. After all, you hosted last year's get-together and this year your family is in the middle of a major remodel job, going all shiplap and such, with brand new hardwood floors that will be installed the week following the feast. Your dining room will be down to the bare subfloors when the turkey and fixins' are served.

When your sister-in-law initiates the conversation with a rather straightforward and demonstrative tone, she chooses these words: "Hey. We need to talk about Thanksgiving. It's not going to work out for me to host so we're going to have to have it at your place. Okay?"

No, you think. *It is not okay.* Everything within you wants to scream it from the top of your lungs. Your sis-in-law is a me-first maximizer. It's usually her way or the highway, and your extended family members routinely capitulate, giving in to her way. Your customary pattern of response would be to agree to host and then stress about the fact that you all will be munching on your green bean casserole and enjoying your pumpkin pie on your lovely, temporary plywood floors. But this year, you decide things will be different. You're not going to mumble and acquiesce. You're going to speak up but do so in a thoughtful and careful manner. So, you whisper a prayer, take a deep breath, and reply.

"Hey, thanks so much for bringing the subject up. I always love when we can get together, and I'm looking forward to Thanksgiving. However, I've been thinking about whether or not it's going to be possible for us to host this year. Sadly, as much as I would love to do it, we are having hardwood floors installed the week after Thanksgiving and our house is going to be torn up in preparation. I just won't be able to give the get-together the setting and atmosphere it requires. How about we do something different this year, if everyone is up for it? We could all eat out. Or maybe I can see if we can reserve the fireside room at my church. I will jump on the family text message thread and let everyone know about our remodeling situation and the fact that you said you can't host either. Then, we can go from there."

Now, such a response will do a few things. First, it will reaffirm to your sister-in-law that you enjoy getting together with her. Bringing into the conversation the fact that the main point is for loved ones to gather might help to diminish any combativeness that may arise.

Second, you are being truthful about your situation without trying to garner pity or sympathy. You are just stating facts. Your dining room—and most likely your kitchen—are going to be in disarray and not an ideal place for a large family gathering.

Finally, you are drawing others into the situation by announcing that you are going to relay all this information to the family. If she is declining to host just because she doesn't want to clean her house, or some other noncrucial reason, telling the entire family will call her on the carpet a bit. Perhaps she will change her mind because she doesn't want to appear to be uncooperative to the rest of the family. But again, you are not trying to spin anything here. You are just giving straightforward facts. And it's best to do that in a manner where everyone can see them at the same time, rather than texting back and forth with individual people. I find our family's group text message thread works as does a private group message on a social media platform such as Facebook or Instagram.

Hopefully, being careful, prayerful, and thoughtful will open up conversation that is loving and honest, as together you all tackle the issue of where Thanksgiving will be celebrated that year. Of course, there are no guarantees. There are some people who simply live to be critical, controlling, and combative; no matter what you say they are not going to give in. In such cases, when they don't want to go along with the majority, I say the majority just marches ahead and makes their plans, letting that person know they are welcome to join in, if they wish. However, if they choose otherwise, that is fine too.

What Honesty Isn't

With all the exploration of just what honesty is, it's important to also cover just what honesty is not. Here are a few misconceptions about exactly what truthfulness is—or more accurately, what it is not.

Being Honest Does Not Mean You Are Unwilling

For those who tend to be helpers and like to be thought of as supportive, being honest about your inability to carry out a task—or your hesitation to take on something else right now because you fear it may overload you—might make you fear that the person doing the asking will think you don't have a willing heart. It's helpful to tell them something along the lines of, "I so wish I could help you out here, really I do. However, it's just not a fit in my life right now. If it were, I would gladly say yes. Unfortunately, the reality of my circumstances dictate that I decline." (Okay. I know that sounds a little formal, but you get it. Feel free to word it your own way.) We can learn to be honest while also sharing our sentiments about how we wish the answer could be different.

Next...

Being Honest about Your Situation Does Not Mean That You Are Incapable

Likewise, when we must decline a request from someone who needs our help, we shouldn't become overly concerned that we are going to be viewed as incapable. A straightforward answer is best, letting the person know this is something you would enjoy doing if it came at a different time, but unfortunately you just don't have the margin in your life right now. Capable people often are asked to help. However, just because you are capable of something doesn't always mean that you are called to do it.

Being Honest about Your Limitations Is Not an Indication That You Are Inept

Don't let your internal thoughts trip you up on this one. Many of us do not answer truthfully when asked to take on a task for fear of looking as though we are inept. We do not need to be skilled in everything. Rather than say yes to a request, and then furiously research how to do it correctly, we can simply answer that the request is a bit out of our league and so someone else will be needed to fulfill the plea.

Being Honest Is Not the Same as Being Mean

Okay, here is a big one among friends. And I'm not going to ever assert that I do this one perfectly, because I find it the most difficult one of all. When someone wants our honest opinion about something they have created, written, chosen for their wardrobe, or selected for their house, we so fear hurting their feelings that we often fudge the truth. It gets even more complicated when they want our opinion about something very personal, like how they are parenting their children or behaving in their marriage.

Because I don't at all want to appear that I am being mean, I'm hesitant to tell the truth. A few practices have helped me over the years in this area. One is a phrase I learned from a friend one day on a shopping trip.

She and I were at the mall with our four daughters back when they were all teenagers and preteens. My friend's youngest daughter brought a scarf over to her mom that she really wanted to buy her for Mother's Day. However, she wanted to make sure her mom liked it before she spent her hard-earned babysitting money on it. It wasn't a pattern or color scheme that my friend liked, let alone would ever wear. But, instead of sweetly smiling and saying, "Sure!" just to appease her daughter, she uttered a phrase that was truthful without being mean. She said, "Well, Brooke. It's not my favorite. Are there any other colors and patterns? You are so great picking out fashion items that I'm sure you can find me a fantastic one."

My mouth just about dropped open. I know it's not an earth-shattering proclamation she made, but to me it was a great life lesson. You can say you don't like something without using super-strong language. She simply said it was "not her favorite." Then she complimented her daughter on her fashion prowess and instilled confidence in her by telling her she knew she could pick out a marvelous scarf for her mom. And actually, she did!

I have learned to use the phrase "It's not my favorite" along with other such comments. "See if you can come up with something different. I'm confident you can." Or, in serious situations, I have resorted to this one: "I'm hesitant to be honest for risk of offending you, but I feel it's best to tell the truth." (I had to practice that one over and over again before uttering it in person!)

In addition to having these go-to phrases, the other practice that has really enabled me to make progress in this area is mentally putting myself in the other person's place. Would I want someone to gush over me, telling me how great my outfit was, if in reality it was not flattering at all on my figure or with my hair and eye color? If I wrote a social media post that was confusing, or made a platter of cookies for someone and they tasted awful, would I want a friend to hide the truth from me? Wouldn't I want to know the truth so that in the future I didn't repeat the same blunder? I could learn to write a more powerful and clear blog post or bake a better batch of goodies by not leaving out the sugar next time (true story!) if a friend simply told me the truth.

We aren't doing our friends and loved ones any favors when we lie to shelter their feelings. If we make it known to them how much we love them—and how we would want someone to be honest with us if the tables were turned—we won't be hurting their feelings. We will be giving them a wonderful gift.

In All Honesty

It's been more than two years since I heard my pastor's assertion that people pleasers often lie. I've calmed down and no longer hyperventilate at the thought of being divulged as a fraud. But honestly, his words made me realize that much of my behavior when interacting with others had indeed been fraudulent. Oh sure, I might have argued that I was twisting the truth in a handful of situations only out of concern for the other person's emotional health. But I would just be adding one more lie to the stack of untruths that was piling up in my life.

I won't paint a picture that learning to untangle the truth from my racing mind and state it in a straightforward manner has been easy. It hasn't. I've been worried I would lose a friend or two. I've been fearful I would offend or upset. And it certainly has been a lot more work to be prayerful, careful, and thoughtful when asked for my opinion about something to be honest rather than shade the truth or, at least, change the subject. However, the difficulty in communicating has paled in comparison to the freedom I now feel.

I am no longer gripped by what I called the greatest lie, the one I subconsciously told myself: that if I were ever truly honest, my friends list would dwindle down to just my husband and the family dog. (And we don't even own a dog!) But this has not been the scenario at all. I actually feel my relationships—whether with people inside my family or friends and coworkers—has significantly strengthened. While I still love to be a cheerleader for others—encouraging them and urging them on toward greater things—the peace of mind that I've gained from my new habit of trying to shoot straight while simultaneously expressing my love and care for others has been one of the greatest areas of growth in my life.

And I've also come to a place where my heart can rest confidently knowing that God longs for me to speak the truth in love; that he doesn't like flattery and hates lying lips. This is just a sublesson in the greater overall degree we are earning—a masters in fearing God rather than humans. Let's stop putting others in the place of God, elevating their opinions about us above him and his view.

And so, were you and I to go out together for a cup of coffee and a quick shopping trip, you can trust that if you pick out a scarf I think looks amazing on you, I will tell you just how gorgeous it makes you look, bringing out the beautiful color of your eyes. On the other hand, if it's more ugly than awesome, you might just hear me begin my response with the words, "Well, it's not my favorite." However, you could trust that *you* are one of my favorites. And because I value our friendship, I'm going to risk being vulnerable and honest, knowing I am doing it both to please God and because I have your best interest at heart.

That, my sweet sister, you can count on. In all honesty.

Truth Bombs for Memorization

An effective way to prevent ourselves from repeating a behavior we have been known for in the past is to memorize a portion of Scripture, or even a single verse, that speaks to this habit. This is certainly the case with the topic of honesty.

Here are some verses on truth-telling that you may want to commit to memory. They can help you pause and realign your thinking with God's before you start to speak an untruth or flatter with your lips. (For your convenience, they are also printed again in the back of the book where they have been designed for photocopying or cutting out to keep in a prominent place, such as your car dashboard, the kitchen sink, a bathroom mirror, or even in an envelope in your purse.)

- "Do not lie to each other, since you have taken off your old self with its practices and have put on the new self, which is being renewed in knowledge in the image of its Creator" (Colossians 3:9–10).
- "Therefore each of you must put off falsehood and speak truthfully to your neighbor, for we are all members of one body" (Ephesians 4:25).
- "LORD, who may dwell in your sacred tent? Who may live on your holy mountain? The one whose walk is blameless, who does what is righteous, who speaks the truth from their heart" (Psalm 15:1–2).
- "Instead, speaking the truth in love, we will grow to become in every respect the mature body of him who is the head, that is, Christ" (Ephesians 4:15).

- "Lying lips are detestable to the LORD, but faithful people are his delight" (Proverbs 12:22 CSB).
- "I know, my God, that you test the heart and are pleased with integrity" (1 Chronicles 29:17).
- "Truthful words stand the test of time, but lies are soon exposed" (Proverbs 12:19 NLT).
- "These are the things you must do: Speak truth to one another; make true and sound decisions within your city gates" (Zechariah 8:16 CSB).
- "Whoever of you loves life and desires to see many good days, keep your tongue from evil and your lips from telling lies. Turn from evil and do good; seek peace and pursue it. The eyes of the LORD are on the righteous, and his ears are attentive to their cry" (Psalm 34:12–15).
- There are six things the LORD hates, seven that are detestable to him: haughty eyes, a lying tongue, hands that shed innocent blood, a heart that devises wicked schemes, feet that are quick to rush into evil, a false witness who pours out lies and a person who stirs up conflict in the community (Proverbs 6:16–19).

Chapter 5

What Digital Is Doing to Us

Real life is what happens when your cell phone is charging.

—ANONYMOUS

Look carefully then how you walk, not as unwise but as wise, making the best use of the time, because the days are evil. Therefore do not be foolish, but understand what the will of the Lord is.

—EPHESIANS 5:15–17 ESV

The delicate sounds of birds chirping and lazy waves gently lapping on the ocean shore softly emitted from my alarm clock, awakening me on a chilly Monday morning in October. I tumbled out of bed, donning my favorite fuzzy bathrobe and commenced my morning routine as I faced another week ahead.

First stop on my routine is the kitchen to fire up my beloved coffee maker. My kids pooled all their money for my birthday last year and purchased me a fancy-pants model that not only makes me a delicious dark-roast java but froths my half-and-half as well. This way, I can sip a custom-made latte without having to venture off to The Blue Owl—my favorite coffee establishment.

That morning, I couldn't wait to wrap my hands around a steaming mug of maple-pecan roast. Hopefully, it would snap the sleepy out of my brain and get me on my way. I glanced down at my cell phone next to the coffee maker where I'd plugged it in the night before. I'd begun the custom of banishing my phone from the bedroom so it couldn't tempt me to tap, swipe, and scroll instead of getting to sleep at a decent hour.

As I disabled the airplane mode, about a half dozen or more notifications began their usual morning dance, gliding down from the top of my screen.

Two family members had texted me since I'd shut off my phone the night before. My daughter needed the address of one of her grandparents in order to send them a birthday card. And my sister-in-law was informing our extended family group text that Mom Ehman had fallen the night before at her assisted living facility but thankfully had only bruises and no breaks.

There were seven private messages on Instagram. Two were from people I know in real life. The other five were from women who follow me on that social media platform because they've read my books or done one of my Bible studies. Included among these private messages were three recipe requests for the autumn squash soup I had posted about making for supper the evening prior. Another woman wanted to know if I would recommend resources for parenting toddlers.

It didn't stop there. Another click revealed a message from someone I used to attend church with—but had not heard nearly a peep from in over five years—asking for help in landing a new job by writing a stellar recommendation for her. And don't even get me started about my email inbox. It too was full of messages that contained tasks people wanted me to perform and actions they desired me to take. This montage of messages threatened to ruin my day almost before it even started.

I knew the stifling feeling of stress that was beginning to weasel its way into my brain was not my phone's fault. My device was just sitting there innocently in its cute bubble gum pink case as these requests bossed their way into my morning. Still, I felt like taking that electronic contraption and chucking it against the kitchen subway tile, smashing it to smithereens. Maybe that would stop the incessant scrolling and make people leave me alone already.

My frustrated feelings that morning were evidence of the ongoing love-hate relationship I have with my phone.

My phone can contain my work and personal calendar amalgamated together on its screen, available for viewing with just a tap of my fingertip? LOVE!

My phone can deliver messages from people who want me to help them with some dilemma they have in their life and help them *right now*! HATE!

My phone can flood my feed with darling pictures of my great-goddaughter, a seven-year-old Ethiopian princess named Naomi. LOVE!

My phone houses my social media accounts—along with their private message features—which allow complete strangers to ask me trivial questions, or to give me unsolicited criticism of everything from my latest hairstyle to my choice of Bible version. HATE!

My phone can help keep me connected with high school and college classmates, letting me know when they've suffered a sadness such as the passing of a parent, or a milestone such as a new job promotion or cross-country move. LOVE!

My phone can interrupt my day, crowding my to-do list with

tasks others dream up for me without my input on whether the assignments are indeed mine to do. HATE!

You get the digital picture, right?

All the People. All the Time.

The dawn of the digital age completely revolutionized how we do life. Sure, it has made so many things easier, like finding directions to an unfamiliar destination or searching for a quick but delicious recipe that will use up that bunch of broccoli hiding in your fridge that is soon to go bad. However, in many ways, it has also been a detriment because everybody and their cousin are granted access to make requests—even demands—on your life.

Go back for a moment to your early childhood days. For most of us, our house was equipped with a landline. And if that landline was not outfitted with an answering machine, it was up to the person calling your house to make the connection with whomever they were wishing to speak. If they dialed your number and got no answer, the burden was on them to call you back at a later time. However, today the script is entirely flipped.

If someone wants to reach you and you don't answer the phone, they simply leave you a voicemail. Or, they don't even have to try to speak to you at all. They can just shoot you a text. Send you a direct message on social media. Fire you off an email. And now, the burden is on you to get back with them to answer their questions or grant their requests.

When all these messages inundate my phone, I feel that I am no longer in charge of the day's to-do list. It's like someone has grabbed the pencil from my hand and scribbled down a whole mess of missions on my list, without any input—and certainly without permission—from me.

The fact that our to-do list gets lengthened is only part of the problem. Almost equally detrimental is the wrong perception others have of our accessibility due to the digital age. People now feel that they have instant access to you. They even think they have instant access to their favorite celebrities! When I was a teenager, if I hoped to get a message to my favorite television star, I had to try to hunt down the address of their fan mail club. Then, I could grab a pencil and craft a note I could drop in a mailbox, whisking it away to them, hoping they might actually read it.

But have things ever changed! Now, with a handy little device in our hands, we can tweet at a celebrity. We can send a direct message to them through Instagram. Or we can post something on Facebook, tagging them and using a clever hashtag as well, all in hopes that they will get our message. And actually, we have a thousand percent better shot of them hearing from us today than we did in the days of snail mail fan letters. Social media is full of interactions between the famous and the everyday Joes and Janes.

Perhaps most aggravating for me has not been this feeling of instant access from strangers. Instead, it is the expected response time people in my real life anticipate when reaching out to me digitally. People assume you are tethered to your phone, having it always on your person. They expect you to instantly respond to any messages they might send you, whether by text or otherwise. Perhaps their expectations in this realm are due to the fact that they themselves are never without their phones. Their life is characterized by a constant interaction with their device. So, they find it quite strange when you do not conduct yourself the same way.

Let's just take text messaging for example. Americans send over twenty-six billion text messages per day. (Yes, billion, with a B!) And on average, the typical American sends and receives ninety-four text messages per day and spends about fifty-five minutes a day just reading and sending these texts.[1]

And just how quickly do the people in your life expect you to respond to one of those digital messages they send you? Well, if it is a client or a boss, and it is during working hours, they expect a response in an hour or less. However, if it is not during working hours and you are texting with either a family member or friend, 95 percent of such texts will be read within five minutes of being sent, with the average expected response time for a text being a mere ninety seconds.[2]

This instant access, combined with the expected rapid response, causes people to become aggravated if they do not get a reply in what they deem is a timely fashion. And the fact that we have an online presence, especially on our social media accounts, has expanded the whole scenario even further.

One day my daughter was spending some time here with us in Michigan, having made the trip up from her home in North Carolina. We were relaxing on the back deck, sipping cold-brew coffee and catching up on each other's lives. She had her cell phone nearby where she'd been taking care of some things for work. She owns a salon and so she still has to troubleshoot from afar when she is on vacation. She'd also just posted a picture to her Instagram account telling how happy she was to be home in the Midwest, grabbing some down time with the fam.

All of a sudden, her phone buzzed. It was a notification alerting her to a Facebook message from someone she'd not had contact with in a few years. She wasn't close to this person, but they were Facebook friends. They wanted to know some information about a close friend of my daughter who was going through a rough time in her marriage and who was most likely getting a divorce. My daughter ignored the message. She was on holiday, devoting time to her family and didn't want to be bothered. But most importantly, she didn't consider her friend's marriage any of this person's business.

She continued to let her phone lie there, planning not to

reply for at least a couple days. However, the curious—and quite persistent—person at the other end of the message would not relent. She messaged her a second time. And then a third. Finally, she said something that had me in disbelief and made my daughter furious.

"Please message me back," she assertively began. And then, the I-can't-believe-she-did-that action that took me by surprise, but which my daughter said has happened to her several times. The person continued by alleging, "I know you are on your phone. I just saw you post on Instagram. I'm waiting for your response. Answer me, please."

What in the world? I could not believe that she started bossing—if not practically bullying—my daughter by stalking her on social media. Since that day, I have noticed this phenomenon in my own digital activities. Because we are broadcasting a constant play-by-play of our days on social media, others know our whereabouts. And they know when we have our phones with us when they see us post. (Or at least they think they do. I use a scheduling app for some of my social media posts so I can preload them on the weekend and then walk away for the rest of the week if I want to.)

Years ago, if a friend wanted to get together on a particular day but you told them you were unavailable, that was usually the end of the story. You could plan to get together at a later date. and hopefully there would not be any hard feelings.

Fast forward to today. One day, a friend might ask you to go out for coffee. You politely decline, telling her you have other plans. But what your friend might not know is that your other plans include having lunch with a different friend. And so, you launch out on that lunch date, completely forgetting the fact that you turned down the coffee date a few hours earlier. Then—as is the habit of many of us on social media—you post a quaint snapshot of your delicious chopped cobb salad nestled next to the grilled portabella sandwich and sweet potato fries your friend is enjoying. You grab the location of the eatery when posting. You also tag your friend in your post adding the hashtag #lunchwithfriends.

Oops.

You polish off your salad and then—as you peruse the dessert menu, trying to decide between the key lime pie or the flourless chocolate cake—your cell phone beeps. It is a text from the gal who wanted to have coffee. She says something snarky, her feelings obviously hurt. And now your heart is housing some anxiety about the anticipated awkwardness of discussing the situation with her. You never meant to hurt her feelings. And obviously, when you posted your picture, you were not even thinking about the fact that your friend followed you on social media and was going to see that you were out to lunch with someone else that day.

Is there a way to avoid offense in this scenario? If the friend desiring the coffee date was not insecure about your friendship— and if you had been upfront with the reason you were declining her invitation, letting her know you already had another lunch date with a friend—it would eliminate the potential for a sticky social media situation. But when insecurities lurk in the heart of another—and you are chronicling your happenings each day on Instagram stories—you might land yourself in a spot where you feel you have some explaining to do.

But are the people in our lives owed any justification from us about our choice of activities? Can't we just live out our days as we wish, regardless if it makes someone else upset, jealous, or even angry? How do we navigate the constant broadcasting of our day's agenda without getting tangled up like those three pairs of wired earbuds you currently have laying in the bottom of your desk drawer? How do we deal with *all the people* who seem to have access to us *all the time* as they observe us living our lives right there in the palm of their hands?

Screen Time Strategies

If we don't come up with strategies for preventing people from coercing us through their digital interactions with us, we will find ourselves being ever so subtly, or even overtly, pressured. Here are a few concepts to consider—and practices to adopt—that will help us navigate the stress we often feel coming by way of our phones.

First . . . okay . . . this may be hard for some of us . . .

Be Honest about Your Own Phone Addiction

I know. I know. You don't think you have an issue with your phone usage. I for sure used to believe that about myself. That was until my friend Lindsey told me about the day she checked her own cell phone usage by way of an app that kept track of it—even down to how many times the phone was touched! Up until then, she had never considered how long she was actually on social media or hopscotching all over the web checking out blog posts and websites. Or even the time she devoted to texting others. When she finally took note of the prior twenty-four hours of activity one evening, she was shocked at how much time that day she had spent on her phone and the hundreds—yes hundreds!—of times she'd picked it up.

And so, inspired by her quest for self-awareness, I decided to not change my habits at all, but to check at the end of the coming week to see how much time I had spent on my phone. (My phone actually keeps track of that internally without any exterior app.) I'm pretty good at limiting myself on Facebook and Instagram, and I spend very little time nosing around on different blogs and websites. But for me, I am lured in by Twitter. I like to check it in the evening before going to bed to catch up on the day's news.

Now, if you had asked me how much time I spent on Twitter each evening, I would have estimated about ten to fifteen minutes. Just enough time to check news outlets to see what is going on in the world. I couldn't believe my eyes when at the end of the week I saw that the average time I'd spent on Twitter each evening was forty-seven minutes. That totals 329 minutes a week! Do the math with me. I was spending five-and-a-half hours a week frittering and Twittering my time away!

This wakeup call compelled me to take two action steps: to set a limit of fifteen minutes on my Twitter app and also to cease taking my telephone into the bedroom before bed. It now spends the night on the kitchen counter where I can no longer see its flashing screen beckoning me to check yet another news article.

Be honest about how much you allow your phone to control you, rather than the other way around.

That leads us to the next suggestion.

Predetermine Some Digital Boundaries

When it comes to real estate property, boundary lines are drawn delineating your property from your neighbor's. It shows the point where your property ends and theirs begins. In relationships, boundaries serve as a personal property line displaying your personal space and just how far someone can venture into it.

I will be the first to admit that I stink at boundaries. Over the years I set up a pattern of behavior that told people in my life I was willing to drop whatever I was doing and help them out. I don't really fault them for overstepping their bounds. I taught them by my behavior just how they could treat me. If I did have any boundaries in place, they were not firm. They were like the thinnest spider web glistening in the morning sun. Easy to see but also a breeze to break through.

When it comes to our cell phones, here's what a boundary might look like: When it's time for your family to have supper, you will place your cell phone in the *Do Not Disturb* mode. This feature allows calls only from those on your "favorites list." You are the one who crafts this list. For me, I have on it the members of my immediate family, all the grandparents, the assisted living facility where my mother-in-law lives, and my direct boss at work in case an emergency should arise. When I place my phone in *Do Not Disturb* mode—from the time I sit down to supper until the next morning when I fire up the coffee maker—all other calls and text messages are silenced. (This feature does allow a call to ring through if two calls come from the same number in less than three minutes. In that way someone with a true emergency can still reach you.)

After a while, people in my life have come to know this boundary I've enacted, and they no longer expect an instant reply. They know I will not see their text message until the next morning. You can also generate an auto-response that will be sent when your phone knows that you are driving in a car. Mine says, "I am driving with my phone's *Do Not Disturb* feature turned on. I will see your message sometime later when I reach my destination and have time to respond. Thanks so much."

Boundaries will help in the area of text messaging. But what about all the places people can find you online? For that I suggest this...

Send Out a Social Media Syllabus
by Your Consistent Behavior

I think we all know the power of social media. It can be used for good: to get a petition rolling to bring about needed change. It can be a fun place for amusement: sending a friend a hilarious video gone viral. Unfortunately, it can also be used for evil: such as bullying kids online. However, did it ever occur to you that your behavior on social media is giving a little lesson to the people you connect with there?

It's true! To prove my point, let me ask you a few questions. Can you think of someone who is on one of your social media accounts—let's say Facebook—who you can count on to always be the first person to like a post or toss up a comment? I know one such person in my extended family. He has a full-time job outside the home, but it appears that he has his phone with him around the clock because no matter when I—or anyone else in the family—posts something, ninety-nine times out of one-hundred, he will be the first to like and/or comment.

But then, think of the opposite. Are there people you connect with on social media who you know rarely like a post or post a comment? In fact, you're rather shocked when you hear from them, which is usually only the obligatory "Happy Birthday" Facebook message they send you every year.

Each of these people has given you their social media syllabus. Just like an instructor—who gives you a clear picture of what to expect during the school year in the syllabus they hand out the first day of class—these people, by their repeated patterns of behavior, have told you precisely what you can expect from them. And you are doing the same with the people in your life.

It will be worth your time to examine your digital doings, seeing if they are adding to the pressure you feel from others. If people have picked up on the fact that you are among the first to dive in and help or to sign up to volunteer, you will become a go-to person when they need something done. If you have given the impression that you are constantly clicking, liking, and commenting, you may irritate someone when they see you have failed to like their post. (I know this is more prevalent with teenagers, but even adults seem to get their nose out of joint if someone doesn't like one of their posts.)

I actually used to be guilty of over-liking posts on social media. Then, Facebook introduced a heart symbol besides its blue thumbs-up as a reaction to a post. A friend of mine said that she was going to be very selective with what posts to which she ever bequeathed a heart. After all, if you are doling them out left and right, it really waters down the meaning of the heart, doesn't it? I now respond and comment way less often and reserve those hearts for only the posts by which I am truly touched.

You may also want to explore putting in place other boundaries and parameters by adjusting your settings in your social media accounts. I used to give at least an hour a week to respond to private messages that I received on my Facebook page. So many of these messages were from people wanting to know if I would promote their multilevel marketing business or feature their side hustle on my website. Others would ask me to help them solve personal problems, even though I am not a licensed trained counselor. Rarely were any of the requests something I needed to know about or was able to help with. I finally came up with a simple solution. I turned off the private messaging feature on my Facebook page. People can still send an email through my website, but I find they are less likely to do so.

Next—oh this one took me some time to adopt . . .

Become Familiar with the Block Feature and Delete Button

If putting parameters in place and sending out a consistent social media syllabus are not enough, we may need to take an even more drastic measure. After lamenting to a friend one day about the many requests I was getting to promote books by people I've never heard of or to feature their products on my website or social media accounts—sometimes multiple messages in a day from the same person—my wise friend looked at me and simply said, "Well, there is a solution. Just delete their comment and do not respond. And if someone is repeatedly harassing you, block them!"

Delete and block? But that seems so extreme! But let me tell you, it has saved my social media sanity. The access people have to you online now has granted them license to annoy—if not downright harass—you. Don't be afraid to use these effective tools if you must.

Next...

Accept the Results of Your Boundaries and Behavior without Feeling Guilty

Okay, sisters, I'm preaching to myself on this one. A few years ago, it was dreadfully difficult for me to take the advice that I am giving you here. While in the majority of instances people understood my boundaries and respected them, some got a tad irritated, if not downright angry, at me. A few of them let me know it.

For instance, there was the woman—someone I didn't even know—who saw me post that I was making cheesy corn chowder for my son and his football teammates and then sent me a message on Facebook asking me for the recipe. I purposely did not respond. It was a day when I was slammed, and I didn't have time to sit and type an entire recipe. Forty-five minutes later, she messaged me again. And then again, another couple hours after that. I still did not respond. And so, she pulled out her secret weapon: her husband. He sent me a message informing me that his wife had reached out to me several times for the recipe and was planning to make it for him for supper that night. He resolutely requested that I kindly give it to her because it was getting to be late afternoon and she needed to get to the grocery store to purchase the ingredients before starting his supper.

Can. You. Believe. This?

The boldness! The nerve! I was flabbergasted. I waited two full days and then responded to them both. I was polite and kind. I thanked the wife for following me and told her I did not have time in my schedule that day to type a recipe. However, I was planning an upcoming post on my blog about my top five favorite fall soups, and I was including that one in the bunch. I told her to stay tuned because the post would be up in a few days. I'm not sure how she felt about my delayed reply because I never heard back from her again. (Gee, I sure hope her poor hubby didn't go hungry that night!)

Other people who were not pleased with my newfound boundaries were individuals I actually knew in real life. One was someone I knew more than twenty-five years ago when I was in high school. I was friends with her sibling, but not so much with her. She was more of an acquaintance. Her message started out, "Hey, sweet friend," which have become words that are very triggering for me. Every "Hey sweet friend" salutation is usually followed by some big ask. It's gets my "ask antennae" up immediately when I read it.

Anyhow, she said she had been following my ministry and career and gushed about how happy she was for me that I had become an author. And then? Then came the ask. Well, actually, it wasn't an *ask* as much as it was a *tell*.

She felt the Lord calling her to write a book. I will not dispute that at all; he very well may have been. What I take issue with was what followed. She said she had been praying about how to break into the publishing industry and God kept bringing my name to her mind. She wanted to get together to "pick my brain," have me help her write a book proposal, and then get it into the hands of an editor. And she confidently pulled the God card, saying it was all his idea in the first place. Who is gonna say no to the Lord himself?

I kept thinking, if it was his idea, why had he neglected to tell me so? I probably over-explained myself to her when I answered. I was kind of new at this thing. But I let her know that I did not have the margin in my life to coach clients one-on-one. Besides, I do that professionally as part of *Proverbs 31 Ministries' COMPEL Writer's Training*, coaching small groups of clients for hire. That's not to say I wouldn't help a friend write a book. I have helped a few who are close friends. (Translation: those who I interact with week-to-week. The ones who bring a casserole when my family is grieving or who I invite over for a backyard bonfire. Not acquaintances I haven't heard from in decades.)

When you put some firm boundaries in place, there's no doubt it will upset some people and you may have to navigate some uncomfortable conversations. However, you will be saving your sanity by monitoring your capacity and using your time wisely. Don't let the guilt get to you. It's usually false guilt anyway, heaped on you by the other person. Make it a matter of prayer and if God is truly calling you to say yes to a request, he will convict you of that, not guilt you into it.

Passing Your Screen Test

The requests that come our way today go beyond the old, "May I borrow a cup of sugar?" from a next-door neighbor of years' past. Now people need us to send them the link, tell them where we purchased something they see on our Instagram post, put our name on the digital sign-up sheet, or—the one I dread the most—repost their cheesy graphic if we "truly love Jesus and are not ashamed of it." The digital age has dawned, giving even more avenues for those who want our time, asking—or even demanding—that we help them.

My prayer for you is this: when you flip open your laptop or swipe the screen on your phone, you will have already put measures in place that will greatly reduce the number of people trying to get you—or even guilt you—to do something. If you aren't intentional to fill your time, there are dozens of others out there waiting to fill it for you. They need only to shoot you a text or send you a message.

Stand strong, yet be pleasant and kind. Put parameters in place that are healthy for your relationships and oh-so-freeing for you. Let's not allow others to tempt us to people-please by the way they digitally treat us.

Chapter 6

How to Be in the "No"

*Learn to say no; it will be of more use to you
than to be able to read Latin.*

—CHARLES HADDON SPURGEON

*"But let your 'yes' mean 'yes,' and your 'no'
mean 'no.' Anything more than this is from the
evil one."*

—MATTHEW 5:37 CSB

My summer of necessary and no was very eye-opening for me. Because I had purposed not to take on anything beyond what was essential for my home, family, and ministry job, it emphasized for me just how frequently I was asked to take on a responsibility, grant a request, or help someone out. I didn't become skilled at articulating the word *no* right away. It was painful at first and took some time to get used to. (Okay. I'm actually still not totally used to it!) But having to say it so much those few months highlighted for me how many opportunities are rapping on our doors, trying to get us to say yes.

It's that coworker who needs help with something that is totally not your area of expertise, but due to your friendship with them, you agree.

It's the relative who just purchased their first home, with six rooms that need painting, and they've never painted before. But because they know that you are a pro at flinging a paintbrush, they wonder if you might make the half-hour drive to their house to help them bang out a room or two.

It's the committee at church that has a spot on it reserved for you, because you are so good at putting on women's events. Or your child's teacher who wants help with the classroom project, or their coach, who needs someone to organize all the after-game snacks for the season. Or it is the neighbor who wants you to feed their cats twice a day for the next week while they're gone, also emptying out their litter box each day.

And then there are the ones that garner your earnest sympathy. Your newly divorced friend who needs a sitter for eight hours on Saturday in order to attend a weekend course at the local community college; she hopes to jump-start her education so she can find a better-paying job. Another friend is organizing a meal train for someone who just had a death in the family. And then your cousin calls; he is setting up a schedule of relatives who can stay overnight with Grandma so she can continue to live in her house rather than move to a senior-citizen apartment complex.

Not only does agreeing to these requests send our stress level through the roof, but it also wipes out any white space in our calendars we might have for more effectively living out our priorities—spending time with God, our families, pursuing a hobby, or just getting some much-needed rest. Every time we say yes to something we shouldn't, we are saying no to something important.

One of the wisest people I know in the arena of when to say

yes and how to say no is my close friend (and the president of Proverbs 31 Ministries) Lysa Terkeurst. She passed along some advice she learned from pastor Louie Giglio in her helpful book *The Best Yes: Making Wise Decisions in the Midst of Endless Demands*: "Whenever you say yes to something, there is less of you for something else. Make sure your yes is worth the less."[1]

Observing Lysa's behavior over the course of more than two decades of friendship has taught me so much about the significance of our simple answers of *yes* or *no* and their ability to not only affect our schedules but our mental health as well. She has accomplished some amazing things in her life, both in her family and her ministry. But being able to observe her up close has shown me none of this is by accident. It is because she knows the power of what she refers to as a small no.

Saying no to the things that we discern—through prayer and the study of God's Word—are ours not to do, frees us up to say yes to the important assignments God has for us. It takes walking closely with God to courageously say yes to what he has called us to do only *after* we have been assured that we are to say no to some lesser things. I've heard Lysa sum this up by advising, "Find that courageous yes. Fight for that confident no."

When we learn to say no with confidence, we free ourselves up to say yes to what God—not other people—is asking us to do.

What Is God's Will?

I find the whole concept of the will of God a rather fascinating topic and one where you can find people all over the spectrum as to its meaning. I also assert that it is an area where people often get tripped up. They find it so mysterious and hard to understand. They so desperately dread making a mistake, taking them off the one perfect path that God has for them. Whether it is what college we should attend, if—or who—we are to marry, how to parent a child or what home to buy, we imagine God sitting up in the clouds, with one perfect—yet somehow extremely complicated—formula for exactly how our life is to go. He has an intricate road map dotted with every single decision we are to make. If we ever make the wrong one, we fall out of line with God's perfect will. But is this really the case? It's no doubt that our decisions are important, but are they so esoteric that they're virtually impossible to figure out?

Do an internet search on the phrase *how to find God's will for my life* and the tens of thousands of results that appear could take you the rest of your life to read! Let's try to uncomplicate things, coming up with a helpful grid for discerning when you should say yes and when it is more beneficial for you to say no, and how this relates to God's will. As always, Scripture holds the key to help us navigate life and situations such as these.

Here are a few questions to ask yourself, along with some passages that help with the answers:

Have I Been Deliberate to Pray about Daily Decision Making in My Life?

Pray in accordance with Romans 15:5–6 which pronounces, "May the God who gives endurance and encouragement give you the same attitude of mind toward each other that Christ Jesus had, so that with one mind and one voice you may glorify the God and Father of our Lord Jesus Christ."

Ask the Father to give you encouragement and grant you endurance. Pray that you would have the mind of Christ in your daily decision making with regards to how it affects not only you but others as well. Petition God for wise choices that will glorify him.

The apostle Paul writes in 1 Corinthians 2:15–16, "The person with the Spirit makes judgments about all things, but such a person is not subject to merely human judgments, for, 'Who has known the mind of the Lord so as to instruct him?' But we have the mind of Christ."

Pray that the Holy Spirit will allow you to make sound judgments rather than ones only based on your own human reasoning.

Next, add these ongoing questions to your daily prayer time with God:

Does This Violate Anything God Has Laid Out in Scripture?

This important pondering will allow you to say no right off the bat in some instances. We should never say yes to actions we know are against God's Word. These might seem rather obvious and don't need addressing, but you would be surprised how many people get themselves entangled in a complete mess because they did not say no to something God forbids in his Word.

For example, does your spouse want you to fabricate some information on your taxes, telling lies that will bring you a greater tax return? Does your coworker ask you to cover for them, lying to your boss about where they are because they know if the truth were found out they would be in trouble? In each of these scenarios, our answers should be clear. God's Word states that lying is wrong. So, we should say no when requested to do so. Oh, I realize that might be easier said than done, especially if you have developed a habit in the past of lying for these people. But we can save ourselves drama or heartache if we refuse to participate in anything that God says is wrong.

Have I Taken Time to Ponder and Pray about This Specific Request?

Sometimes giving a wrong answer is due to the fact that we responded to the request right away, without taking time to mull it over and asking God for his clear direction. By doing so, we can help steer ourselves on the right path rather than run off course because we answered too soon. Proverbs 29:20 echoes this thought:

> Do you see someone who speaks too soon?
> There is more hope for a fool than for him. (CSB)

And the book of James—one of the most practical books in the Bible as well as one of my favorites—also urges us to not be so quick to pipe up:

> My dear brothers and sisters, take note of this: Everyone should be quick to listen, slow to speak and slow to become angry ... (James 1:19)

When we pause and pray, we are better positioned to make the best choice. And communicating with God through prayer can help take the anxiousness and worry out of the decision-making process when we fear we might answer wrongly.

Paul writes in Philippians 4:6–7:

> Do not be anxious about anything, but in every situation, by prayer and petition, with thanksgiving, present your requests to God. And the peace of God, which transcends all understanding, will guard your hearts and your minds in Christ Jesus.

When does this passage suggest that we go to God in prayer? In every "situation." And believe me, many of the requests that come our way requiring a yes or no answer can lead to us finding ourselves in some serious situations, trapped by our affirmative answer.

So, stop, ponder, pray, and then also ask yourself if you've attempted this old-but-effective practice . . .

Have I Laid Out a Pro and Con List?

Okay, I know this sounds like a decision-making practice your mom taught you in the seventh grade when you were trying to decide which sport to try out for, but it is actually a very helpful exercise. Whether you do it digitally or the old-fashioned way on a notepad with a ball-point pen (I have some pretty pink and aqua pens I purchased just for this purpose!), write the request, opportunity, or question across the top of the paper. Then, just underneath, on one side jot "Pros" and on the other side "Cons," forming two columns.

List anything that pops into your mind that fits in either of these categories when you think of saying yes to the opportunity, request, or question. This isn't an exercise you're going to finish in five minutes. Spend at least twenty to thirty minutes contemplating as you create your lists. Then, drop the legal pad and pen and walk away for twenty-four hours.

Revisit the lists the next day and read what you've written, adding any additional items in either column as you do. Often seeing the pluses and minuses of a situation written out in black and white (or in my case, in aqua and pink!) right there before you can help you come to your conclusion.

If you feel you are leaning toward a yes in the situation, next contemplate this:

Have I Factored in What Saying Yes to This Will Do to My Other Roles and Commitments?

Each time we say yes to a commitment, we are plopping a new responsibility on our plate. Unless we have a lot of room on the plate, which most of us don't, we are going to need to rearrange some things—or even perhaps remove some things—to make way for the new request. Seriously consider what saying yes will do to the things to which you have already committed. We often overestimate how much we can handle, not giving ourselves an accurate picture of what the new responsibilities will do to the plates we are already spinning in life.

When thinking through this aspect of the situation, also be sure to ask yourself the following:

Might I Be Able to Grant the Request If I Delegated Something Else?

Your answer does not always have to be no. Sometimes we *are* being called to take on a new endeavor. If after prayer and reflection, you feel the Lord leaning you toward answering yes—but you're not sure how you are going to fit the new obligation into your already demanding life—consider that it may be time to bow out of something in which you are currently involved. Keep in mind, of course, that if you have made a commitment, you will want to see it through until the designated time the obligation ends. God may be calling you to say yes to something new by saying no to something that he no longer desires for your life.

Also, ask yourself this . . .

Have I Solicited Input from Others Who Are Prayerful and Have My Best Interests at Heart?

This is no time for a solo act. Enlist the prayers and advice from mature Christians you know, soliciting help in your decision making. By having them seek God for answers, and sharing their thoughts with you as they do, you'll gain insight and realize decisions more easily.

I love the concept of getting advice from others that is laid out in the Amplified Version of Proverbs 15:22–23:

Without consultation and wise advice, plans are frustrated,
But with many counselors they are established and succeed.

A man has joy in giving an appropriate answer,
And how good and delightful is a word spoken at the right
moment—how good it is!

If our aim is to give an appropriate answer—which will ultimately bring joy—we must seek out wise advice and solid spiritual consultation.

And finally, reflect on this...

Once I Have Figured Out My Decision—But Not Given It Yet—Have I Honestly Asked Myself If Pleasing Another Person Had Any Role in It?

If it has, you will need to admit this, be brave, and perhaps change your answer.

Okay, let's say you have walked yourself through this process and you are absolutely certain you should decline the request. What is the best way to go about doing that, being completely honest but also keeping your relationship with the other person intact and in good standing?

Let's start with a little lesson from the gridiron.

Learning to Play Defense

Our youngest son started at defensive end on his state champion football team. It might seem more thrilling to play on offense. Just imagine being the one to score a touchdown or the quarterback who makes a last-minute "Hail Mary" throw to a receiver, who then dives into the end zone and wins the game. But the truth is, as many games in the blue-and-gold Ithaca Yellowjackets'

14–0 senior season were won by strategic and strong defense as through dazzling and show-stopping offense.

If we want to learn to rack up a winning record in the people-pleasing game, we are going to need to learn to play defense, putting in place boundaries and strategies that will help us not be so prone to giving in when we should be standing firm. Here are a few that have worked for me quite nicely. First . . .

Fly the Caution Flag Early

People who are adept at getting what they want from others—whether they are of the pushy personality type or more of a soft, yet manipulative sort—are experts at reading your body language and interpreting the phrases you utter. Learn to fly the caution flag early, cluing them in to the fact that you will not say yes immediately but will carefully contemplate all ramifications of saying yes before giving your answer. If they sense an open crack in your resolve, they will seize it as an opportunity to further play on your emotions, your kindheartedness, or your generous spirit in order to get exactly what they want. However, if they start to sense from you—in a non-wimpy way—that you cautiously contemplate your decisions before responding, they may not be so quick to ask.

Don't Give a Litany of Excuses

There is no need to launch out a long list of excuses, trying to defend yourself. I have been guilty of this way too many times. Keep the main thing the main thing. Give them a straightforward answer as to why you are saying no, including only the necessary info. Don't elaborate. You don't owe them a detailed explanation. Focus, sister, focus! (That was me giving myself a pep talk about a "no" answer I need to give someone later today!)

In order to help with this endeavor, begin by applying this next point . . .

Arm Yourself with Some Gentle, but Strong, Go-to Statements

This can be so effective! No doubt you've had times when, in your mind, you knew what you wanted to say (just like I did when my friend asked if her son could stay with us during certain days that fateful summer). However, there was a disconnect when you attempted to download the thoughts you were thinking and string them into coherent sentences that your lips could actually speak! If you sense caution, reluctance, or outright resistance to what you are being asked to do, having an arsenal of preplanned responses sure comes in handy.

Here are a few suitable statements to have in your repertoire of responses. Once you get one of these declarations out of your mouth, you can finish the sentence based on the current situation at hand.

- "While I would love to help, I simply don't have the bandwidth right now to be of any assistance."
- "I really care about you and what you are experiencing. However, I'm not able to carve out any time to help with this without dropping some balls at work or at home so I have to say no."
- "I can see you clearly need some help, but my saying yes would actually be detrimental because I can't give this the focus it requires and deserves."
- "God's been dealing with me about taking on too many responsibilities outside of my home. Therefore, I'm in a season of not taking on anything new right now. Thanks for understanding."
- "I'm so sorry to hear about your situation. Although I am not able to help to remedy it, I will be praying that you find the perfect person to help."

This last one leads to our next go-to strategy . . .

Offer an Alternative Solution or Two

We should be concerned about the situations that loved ones in our lives bump up against. But we can't always swoop in and be their savior. (Jesus has already taken that job!) However, if you know in your heart you should not be the one to help with their situation, you can still help them out by suggesting an alternative solution or two.

If time allows, offer to brainstorm with them others who might be able to help. Talk through the situation with them to see if you can invent another way to tackle the problem at hand that might not require someone else's assistance. If you end up with a little down time—such as waiting at the doctor's office or the DMV—do a little research online about their dilemma. Then text them the links that you find as a way to help, without taking on a major role. Help solve the problem *with* the person rather than *for* them.

Alright. This next one is a one-sentence sermon I often preach to myself.

Remind Yourself That Every Need Is Not Necessarily Your Call

This idiom is one a friend empowered me with years ago when all my children were small, and I was a stay-at-home mom. Due to the fact that I didn't have an outside job at the time, countless people came to me wanting help with their project or for me to solve their problem, since they surmised I must've had loads of time on my hands.

Back then I had a major problem of taking on other people's problems. A wise friend taught me to remember that every need is not necessarily my call. Does my friend have a need? Sure, she does. But that does not mean I am the one to help alleviate it. And, when I attempt to meet their need—when I don't really feel called by God to do so—I am taking the blessing away from the person God meant to meet the need in the first place.

We need to discover through prayer, studying Scripture, and relying on the wise counsel of mature Christians in our life, exactly which needs are our calls and which are just supposed to be on our prayer lists. Reminding yourself that not every need is your particular call can serve as a powerful means of busting out of the prison of people pleasing.

Speaking of prison, here's another one . . .

Stop Posting Bail

Some of us are rescuers. Our friend makes a string of unwise decisions that lands them in the middle of a mess, and then they turn to us. We don our helper cape and insert ourselves into the situation, ready to rescue them once again. Stop posting bail! Their situation is not your fault nor is it your responsibility. Even if it's not something morally questionable but is due to a lack of planning on their part, you don't have to be the one to come in and save the day. Remind yourself to quit posting bail and acting as rescuer by repeating this truth to yourself: *A lack of past planning on their part does not warrant a current emergency on my part.*

And finally . . .

Realize You Can Still Say Yes to the Friendship without Needing to Say Yes to Their Requests Every Time

Frequently, those of us who like the approval and commendation of others wrongly assume that if we say no to a friend, we are weakening—and perhaps even damaging—the friendship. But that is not the truth! We can still say yes to a friendship without saying yes to every request that friend makes of us.

Make it your goal to have touchpoints of love and kindness outside of the conversations that have to do with their appeals for help. Send them a handwritten card on their birthday. Text them an encouraging Bible verse or quote that you think might speak to their soul. Send them a gift card to a local coffee house or favorite shop on a random day just to show them you appreciate their friendship.

You can build strong bonds with a friend in so many ways beyond just swooping in and remedying their every need. And if they are a true friend at heart, they will understand that there are times you simply must answer "no."

The Curse of Capability

We smart, strong, and able-to-multitask women have been cursed. Oh, I don't mean some woman in a black pointy hat literally pronounced a hex on us. But we've been cursed, nonetheless. And what is this ill-fated jinx of which we are victims?

Wonder Women

People watching our lives have noticed that we seem proficient at handling a lot. We juggle responsibilities at work and home and appear to do it with ease. And so, when they need help on a project or in a situation, where do they go? To us, of course! After all, we are so capable. So confident. So competent. But this curse of capability—when not directly dealt with head-on—can cause us oh-so-much distress, putting strains on our time and our relationships.

What has helped me more in this area than anything is a concept a wise friend introduced to me years ago. I was a young mom of three children, all under the age of six. But boy did I give off the vibe of capability. Rarely saying no to a request, I was involved in things in my church, community, and extended family to the degree that I barely had time for my fanny to hit the couch unless I was nursing the baby.

It was during this season that a friend articulated a nine-word decree that has been a beacon of guidance for me in the area of overcommitment. When lamenting to her about all the many responsibilities I had—and how I wasn't sure I was ever going to get everything finished—she let me in on a little guideline she had in her own life, one that kept her from taking on too much and losing her mental stability. It is this. Are you ready?

Don't Take on More Than You Can Pray For

Huh? I asked her to explain further. In her gentle and calm way, she explained that with every new commitment came new people and situations that would make their way into her life. Because she was a woman of prayer, naturally she would want to pray for these people and to take the circumstances surrounding each situation to the Lord. And so, she decided that if she did not have the time to take on the responsibility of praying for all that would come her way due to the new commitment, she simply said no.

If her prayer life was overloaded due to other commitments and family situations, she did not want to be stretched too thin spiritually. Her inability to take on praying for the new commitment necessitated that she politely decline. She felt no need for any further explanation. She's simply smiled and sweetly told them that her answer was going to have to be no.

Holding fast to your convictions in situations of potential overcommitment can be an uncomfortable experience. People won't understand. They may pressure you. They may pout if you don't acquiesce. And in some instances, your friendships may be affected. (Although, if someone does not truly understand your need for saying no once you've thoroughly prayed it through and made the decision that is best for you and your family, how good of a friend were they in the first place?)

Sticking to your guns and remaining consistent will take focused discipline. And loads of wisdom. And perpetual perseverance. But God is more than willing to give us all of this. Just remember, you don't owe others an excuse for why you said no, but you will owe God an explanation for why you said yes.

What Your Yeses Have Cost You

Our lives are a series of decisions. Lots of decisions. In fact, experts in the field of psychology estimate that we make about two thousand decisions an hour while awake—about one decision every two seconds! This adds up to about thirty-five thousand per day![2] Lest you think that an overexaggeration, in the past thirty seconds you may have decided to scratch a mosquito bite, take a sip of water, look out the window to see what car was driving by so fast, check the time, twist your earring out of habit, and turn to the page you are now reading.

Our wisdom—or lack thereof—when it comes to making decisions greatly shapes our current days, not to mention our future. If we want to build a life that pleases God and doesn't stress us out with overcommitment, we need to be intentional about carefully weighing each decision before we make it. This way, we can live in what my friend Lisa calls "no-regret living."

Lisa is a coworker of mine and one of the most purposeful people I know. She's really wise and careful with making decisions. I've learned so much from her not only about ministry but about life in general.

One day last year, I was discussing with her my stage of life, which is often referred to as the sandwich years—that time where you're toggling back and forth between caring for and launching your children into the world as well as caring for your aging parents. I shared with her the frustration I was feeling over trying to tend to all my responsibilities while also tackling my tasks of ministry. Lisa knows me well and she is very familiar with my tendency to take on way more than I should. In fact, about every three years it seems my plate is so full it's going to flop. And so, I go through a time of scraping off responsibilities and reevaluating, making sure the things I put back on the plate are only the ones God would have for me.

As she and I were discussing this, she introduced me to this concept of "no-regret living," a concept she'd learned from a mentor of hers. Lisa says,

> You can do it all ... *just not all at once.* If we want to live a "no-regret" life, we have to realize that it requires self-leadership to prioritize our choices based on our season. Just like the milk in your fridge, your life has time-stamped seasons. Not all of the decisions you make will remain available to you for an unlimited period of time, like rocking babies, visiting aging parents and even some career and educational opportunities.

She then suggests,

> Do a brief review of your current time-stamped opportunities and prioritize them. The best question to ask for a no-regret life is: "What does this season require of me?" The answer to this question may be "I want to drive carpool for my middle schoolers because next year they will have their driver's license." Or it may be "I am going to set aside every Friday night to visit

my parents because those Friday nights are numbered, and I don't want to waste one of them." We don't stumble our way into a no-regret life, we choose our way into it. What will you choose today?

Such prudent advice! When we make a poor decision—saying yes when we should say no—we must be honest about what our yeses have cost us. They cost us time. They cost us calmness of mind. They may cost us visits forfeited with those we love most. They sometimes cost us friendships that are true and genuine and replace them with false ones instead—friends who only seem to like us for what we can do for them. Mostly, these yeses cost us peace as we wrestle in our hearts with the regret of allowing other people to fill our time for us, rather than intentionally loading up our agendas with only what God wants us to do.

While it is a noble gesture to want to be helpful, accommodating, and reliable, sometimes being too nice allows others to take advantage of us. It's time we stood up for ourselves, not in a narcissistic way but in a healthy way. One that puts pleasing God as our greatest goal and loving others secondary.

I know it won't be easy, but in order to reach this goal, I'm going to ask you to do something at which you most likely aren't skilled. It may feel strange and uncomfortable. It may even feel wrong and selfish. But it's not. It's crucial and necessary. You and I are about to explore this foreign, but needed, concept. Are you ready?

It's time you started actually thinking about yourself for once. Oh, not in a self-centered manner, looking out only for number one. It's time you made life more about you because, the truth is, it's really all about how *you* follow Jesus.

Seven "Stop It!" Statements for People Pleasers

Here are some go-to phrases to mull over, and even commit to memory if you wish. They will help you realign your thinking when you start to wander down the path of people pleasing. (For your convenience, they are also printed in the back of the book on page 191, designed for you to photocopy on card stock and cut out so you can keep them in a prominent place where you are sure to see them often.)

- *Every need is not necessarily your call.*
- *Don't take on more than you can pray for.*
- *Their happiness is not your assignment.*
- *You don't need their permission to do God's will.*
- *Stop making their feelings your responsibility.*
- *You don't owe them an excuse for why you said no, but you will owe God an explanation for why you said yes.*
- *You can still say yes to the friendship while saying no to a friend.*

Chapter 7

It's Not about You (But Sometimes It Should Be)

You teach people how to treat you by what you allow, what you stop, and what you reinforce.
—TONY GASKINS JR.

He said to them, "Come away by yourselves to a remote place and rest for a while." For many people were coming and going, and they did not even have time to eat.
—MARK 6:31 CSB

My friend and I grabbed coffee at a local cafe on a lovely spring afternoon. It was just getting warm enough here in the Midwest to be able to enjoy a little sunshine outside while we nursed our beverages, hoping to make them last. I've been eager to try out this new local business, known for lacing their luscious lattes with natural oils and organic half-and-half, rather than artificial pumps of flavoring and fake creamer. The mocha orange latte did not disappoint.

We first got the chitchat out of the way, each of us catching up on the normal subjects, such as what was happening with work and what each of our children was currently up to. It was then I discerned my friend was distressed about an upcoming event. She mentioned that a relative was going to be coming to stay with her for a few weeks. In no way did I sense she was looking forward to the visit. In fact, everything from the tone of her voice to her body language told me she wished she could somehow back out of hosting this person all together. For ease of explanation, we'll call this dreaded guest cousin Claire and we'll refer to my friend as Madi.

I leaned in and listened, letting her unload her racing thoughts. I was curious as to why spending a string of days with this family member was something she dreaded so profusely. It turns out she had more than one reason to be so apprehensive. Seemingly charming on the outside, cousin Claire had a lot of history with Madi when she behaved in a manner contrary to what she portrayed to the world at large. Behind the scenes, cousin Claire's charm gave way to criticism, manipulation, and an ocean of self-centeredness.

First, she always wanted her drop-in visits to happen during a time that was convenient for her. She seemed to care little about what was happening at the home of her host. In fact, she rarely ever inquired as to whether her planned dates were convenient for Madi. But Madi would not speak up. Instead, she used whatever vacation time she had left that year to take time off whenever Claire blew into town.

When visiting, Claire seemed to rattle off a long list of complaints. Everything from the toilet paper not being up to her standards, to the position of the television in the living room not being most convenient for her to watch her soap operas while sipping coffee in the most comfortable chair in the room, to the thread count of the sheet sets in the guest bedroom not being high enough.

However, the criticism wasn't just of my friend's accommodations. Claire seemed to enjoy criticizing other family members and their life choices. She could take a simple discussion on a totally unrelated topic and somehow transition it to a member of the extended family. Once she had switched the direction of the discussion, she would nitpick every tiny detail of the extended family member's life or vilify and malign them for choices they were—or were not—making. Not content to continue her bad-mouthing alone, she would often ask my friend her opinion, or try to get her to agree with her by saying, "You know what I mean, right?" or "Don't you agree?"

These unpleasant conversations were only half of the problem. The other half was how cousin Clare expected to be treated during the visit. She gave off the impression that she anticipated being waited on hand and foot. Apparently, her knowledge of how to run a coffee maker or scramble a few eggs for breakfast had gone completely out the window the moment she stepped foot in my friend's house. Claire never lifted a finger to prepare any of the food nor to clean up when a meal was finished. She wanted to be carted around town, whether shopping or sightseeing or being taken out to dinner. Rarely did she inquire about my friend's plans for the day—such as doctors' appointments or commitments at church. She behaved as if *her* agenda trumped anything else sweet Madi might need to do. In fact, she seemed a bit horrified when my friend mentioned that she couldn't accommodate running her to the mall or the local museum.

I sat with my own sense of horror as I listened to what a demanding person cousin Claire was. And I wondered why Madi just didn't tell her no when the conversation came up about another visit. But as Madi and I talked further, I realized it was hard to say a big no to the request for a visit when she had set up a pattern over the years of not saying the little nos when interacting with Claire.

Because Madi had not said no when asked...*um*...*er*...told about the dates cousin Claire said she was coming, but instead took vacation days to accommodate the visit, she set herself up for future visits to be on Claire's timetable, not hers.

Because Madi had not said no to listening to the criticism of other family members over the years, cousin Claire thought she found an eager audience anytime she wanted to gossip or criticize.

Because she had not said no when feeling the pressure to cater to her cousin every time she was in her house, Madi had set up an expectation that she would play both maid and butler whenever this relative was in her home.

All of these failures to say no—and my friend's wrong thinking that doing so wasn't very nice—amalgamated into the perfect storm of dysfunction. Although Madi absolutely dreaded hosting this person, she felt powerless to put down her foot and either stop the stay altogether or at least put some parameters in place for what behavior of her cousin's she would—and would not—tolerate during a visit.

I know this example is a rather extreme one, but I tell it for a reason. When we repeatedly give in to the wishes of others—without ever sharing our true feelings or standing up for ourselves—we teach them how to treat us, paving the way for their future bad behavior. We wrongly think that we must always be nice. And being nice translates to not telling the truth, rarely factoring our emotional health into the situation, and then failing to say no, which ultimately leads to us being miserable.

The High Price of Nice

The act of being nice has been asked of us since we were tots. Who of us doesn't remember our parents telling us to "play nice" with our siblings or our kindergarten teacher correcting a misbehaving student, chiding them, "That's not very nice!"? Being nice is expected of schoolyard kids, adult citizens (well, maybe not on social media!), and especially of Jesus-loving Christians. But is nice what we are commanded to be in Scripture?

A quick online search of the three translations I use most often when studying and teaching the Bible—the ESV, CSB, and NIV versions—yielded not one solitary result when searching for the word *nice*. You can find some related words such as *kind*, *gentle*, or *loving*. But *nice*, it appears, has left the church building.

Now this doesn't mean that an aspect of being nice is not commendable. Of course, we don't want to be rude. Insensitive. Downright nasty. Nice as it relates to being polite and tactful is certainly behavior we should exemplify. But when our nice goes off the rails, we adopt a persona that ushers in much grief.

Let's just think about Jesus for a moment. Would he be characterized as a "nice guy"? Our perfect Savior—who was fully God and fully man—came to earth to show us the way to live. Did he, by his behavior, show us that the most crucial thing we should be known for is being nice?

Sharon Hodde Miller, author of the book *Nice: Why We Love to Be Liked and How God Calls Us to More*, put it this way:

> Jesus was loving. He was gracious. He was forgiving. He was kind. But he was not nice. He was a man who would leave the 99 sheep to rescue the one, but he was also totally unafraid of offending people. Jesus understood the difference between graciousness and personal compromise, between speaking

truth and needlessly alienating people. Rather than wear a shiny veneer, he became the embodiment of rugged love. This, not niceness, is what we are called to.[1]

Our desire to be known as a nice guy—or rather a nice girl—urges us to keep the peace at all costs and to rarely let our true feelings show, because such behavior will please others. But is nice what we should be aiming for? And, when we achieve the status of "Nicest Person of the Year," what is it doing to our relationships as well as to our own mental, spiritual, and even physical health?

Elevating the desire to be nice at all costs sparks some interesting happenings in our brains. There are studies that indicate that something unpleasant happens in our minds when we disagree with another person or fail to do what a superior is asking us to, whether it is an outright request or just a subtle suggestion we gather from their behavior.

In the 1950s, social psychologist Solomon Asch conducted an extensive research study as part of the Asch Conformity Experiments. These experiments had as their goal observing and documenting what happens to an individual when he or she either goes along with, or against, what their peers think.

Participants were placed in a brain scanner and then read a series of statements they were told were either from students who were their peers or educators who were their professors. It was anticipated that the experiment participants would be reluctant to disagree with a professor since they were in a position of authority. Surprisingly, it made no difference if the person who made the statement was a peer or a prof. The results showed that the participants experienced similar discomfort when disagreeing with a classmate.

Brain scans showed a network of brain regions were notably active during the rare moments "people pleasers" would disagree. The medial prefrontal cortex, which mediates decision-making, and the anterior insula, involved in the experience of social emotions, bodily sensations, among others, showed more activity than other regions. Previous studies have linked these regions to the experience of cognitive dissonance, or the uncomfortable feeling of holding two contradictory beliefs. In other words, those who dislike to disagree tend to experience worse cognitive dissonance when confronted with beliefs they don't agree with compared to their peers. The researchers suspect this is accompanied by heightened mental stress and discomfort. This suggests sensitivity to mental stress is linked to an increased vulnerability to influence.[2]

This research—and other similar experiments I found—concludes that often we go along to get along, being overly nice, simply to avoid mental stress. However, what we often don't realize is that our being extremely nice—taking on too many responsibilities or voicing an untruth that might come back to haunt us later—may cause us greater mental stress in the future than it would in the present moment if we would just be honest with our thoughts and feelings.

Have you ever volunteered to stay late to clean up from an activity at your child's school or at church, thinking it was the right and nice thing to do? However, the event was on a day when you had a crazy busy evening, with kids to get in bed, piles of laundry that had stacked up, and a big project at work the next morning for which you were still preparing. Your being nice by offering to be on the cleanup crew completely threw off your evening routine, causing you to stay up late to finish the laundry and prepare for your work project which mentally stressed you out. Regardless, you agreed to take on the task in order to avoid the mental conflict you would've experienced if you'd stayed silent while knowing there was a need and that others expected you to jump in and meet it.

What other nice responses have cost you peace of mind? Did you offer to keep your friend's puppy for the weekend, even though you are not an animal lover and are slightly allergic to pet dander? However, you knew she was having difficulty finding someone and so you thought the nice thing to do was to offer. Now you will spend your weekend off stuck at home and sneezing. But you *will* retain your "super nice friend" status, which to you is more important than avoiding the mental stress and constant wheezing you'll get by acting as a pet hotel.

My friend Meredith recently gave the keynote message at a virtual conference I attended. She echoed what researchers have found when in her talk she said, "Our brains are hardwired to protect ourselves from things that might hurt us and gravitate towards things that create positive feelings for us." So, we make a blink response, choosing what at first feels pleasant and positive because it will maintain our status of being known as nice, not realizing the future mental tension that lies ahead.

Mental tension is not the only cost we incur by being known as a perpetually nice person. We forfeit our time, which is one of our most important commodities. All of our offers of help, our periods of pitching in and rolling up our sleeves to tackle the task, or our failure to be honest about our current availability when someone wants to talk—they all fill our precious time with actions that retain our reputation as nice but that prevent us from real work we should be doing or leisure time we might have enjoyed.

Craving the title of nice has other consequences relationally. We may think it elevates ourselves in the eyes of others. Perhaps it has, when it comes to people needing our assistance or wanting us to agree with them. But it can cost us relationally with our own families. I've seen firsthand how being too nice—almost becoming a doormat for friends, fellow church members, coworkers, and others—can do just that.

Years ago, I had three close friends who were going through unwanted divorces all at the same time. In each situation, there was infidelity on the part of their spouses. My heart was cracked in two as I thought about these friends and the upheaval they were experiencing in their families. I desired to be supportive and encouraging as they walked this unfamiliar path and helped their children adjust to their family's new reality.

Often these friends wanted to call me to process something new they had discovered about their spouses now not-secret affair. Or, they wanted my opinion about what was happening legally with the divorce proceedings. Sometimes they just needed a shoulder to cry on. And so, they picked up the phone and dialed my number.

Since I longed to support them, I surmised that it was the nice and *right* thing to do to answer the phone any time they called, night or day. I would drop what I was doing with my family to provide a listening ear for my friends. I'm not exaggerating when I say that, between all these friends, I was easily getting nearly two dozen calls per week. I thought it would be unkind if I didn't pick up. After all, I was a stay-at-home mom homeschooling my kids, who were perfectly capable of continuing their schoolwork for a few minutes while I lent a listening ear.

But later, the subject of my new twenty-four-hour crisis hotline came up in my family. My husband really didn't know about it because most of the calls occurred during the day when he was at work. But my children did not hold back in expressing their views.

One of them said, "Mom! You are always on the phone with _____." They were obviously upset by the constant interruptions in our day. They said that often they had a question about their schoolwork, but I had slipped away to another room, or out on the back deck, in order to take my friend's urgent call.

In my mind, I tried to rationalize, reasoning that since they were still children, they just weren't very ministry minded. Didn't they see that my friend needed me right then? Or that Mrs. _____ was soon to lose her status as a Mrs. and she needed some emotional support?

A few days later, I finally decided to do what I should have done all along: take the whole situation to the Lord. I was pretty sure he would give me a slick solution to get my kids on the same page. However, that was not the case at all.

After time in prayer, I became convinced that my habit of always picking up the phone was a detriment to each of my friend's relationship with Christ. They would call. I would answer. They could easily run to me for support, perspective, and advice. But my constant availability was actually preventing them from running to God, to whom they should have headed in the first place.

Our mental peace of mind. Our time. Maybe even our family relationships. Yes, the price of nice is costly. We suffer when we make it our ultimate goal. Sharon Hodde Miller put it perfectly when she wrote, "Niceness is like any good or neutral thing, which becomes a broken thing when it becomes an ultimate thing."[3]

Okay. I'm convinced now. Nice should not be our utmost aspiration. So, just what is a sweet, accommodating Jesus-loving girl supposed to do?

Putting Up Parameters

We've touched on boundaries a little bit when it comes to saying no to others. And certainly, letting others know by our actions that we've enacted clear and measurable boundaries is important in dealing with the disease to please. These barriers and guardrails alert others to exactly what type of behavior we will welcome, tolerate, or refuse to allow.

Remember, not everyone will be happy about the boundaries you put in place. However, it is done both for your mental and physical health and for their benefit as well. Dr. Henry Cloud, an expert on boundaries, describes it this way:

> When we begin to set boundaries with people we love, a really hard thing happens: they hurt. They may feel a hole where you used to plug up their aloneness, their disorganization, or their financial irresponsibility. Whatever it is, they will feel a loss. If you love them, this will be difficult for you to watch. But, when you are dealing with someone who is hurting, remember that your boundaries are both necessary for you and helpful for them. If you have been enabling them to be irresponsible, your limit setting may nudge them toward responsibility.[4]

Boundaries are actually a blessing. Put them in place and watch them work. Your relationships will be healthier in the long run. Of equal importance is having internal parameters in our own mind; restrictions we will adhere to that can prevent us from going overboard with the nice that is wreaking havoc on our peace of mind, our schedules, and our family's lives.

Here are some internal parameters to help us stop offering to save the world and start running our decisions by God before we act.

First, something I learned back in that high school journalism class.

Don't Bury the Lead

This term originated in the early days of newspaper. When penning their articles, reporters were to keep the focus of the piece on the main topic, typically the topic that was promised in the headline. However, sometimes an article gets muddled up with secondary and superfluous facts that don't really pertain to the main subject. This is called burying the lead. (Originally it was lede, not lead. Lede means the first section or sentence of a news article.) An effective news article keeps the lead at the forefront rather than buried a few paragraphs in.

We experience this phenomenon while interacting with others when we bury our no answer under a haystack of nice. You may start out a conversation by saying how much you want to help, or empathizing with the situation in which someone finds themselves. However, the more we ramble, the more we bury the lead. And then, we barely let it bubble to the surface at all! Instead, we have been trapped by our intro and now feel powerless to decline the invitation or say no to their wish.

Instead, keep the lead at the forefront. If you really sense that your answer is supposed to be no, *start out with that* rather than burying your lead. Begin with something like, "I'm so sorry that I won't be able to help you out. However, . . ." And *then* give your reasons for declining. Still empathize with them. You can display concern and care without rushing in and rescuing. Leading off your response with your clear no can help keep you from taking on something you weren't meant to do.

How about this next guideline, which many of us rarely succeed at doing?

Wait Until You're Asked for Help

People pleasers serve as an army of Volunteers of America. Or Europe. Or wherever it is that you live. We are the first to raise our hands to chip in. We are the ones who volunteer to help and serve. Having a servant's heart is a wonderful thing. We should be looking for opportunities to assist others and help get things done in our schools, churches, and communities. But let's not be guilty of overserving.

You don't have to always be the one to volunteer. Try not signing up for anything for the next six months. Wait until you are asked. And then, when you are, decide before answering if it is really something God is placing in your life as an opportunity to serve. You don't have to check the box and hit send, volunteering every time you know there is a need.

Volunteering is only a slice of the problem. The other problem is this . . .

Stop Letting Others "Volun-Tell" You for Tasks

Unfortunately, when we have announced to others by our behavior that we are overly helpful and servant hearted to a fault, they start to "volun-tell" us without our input. We have taught them how to treat us. So naturally they think we won't mind one bit if they go ahead and sign us up in the slot they have open.

You may have to venture out of your comfort zone, but be bold. Politely and firmly tell them that you understand they need help, but you never agreed to offer yours, so you are going to politely refrain from assisting.

It's one thing to be helpful. It's another thing altogether to be a doormat, allowing people to push you around, always assuming that you will step up. Stop letting people in your life volun-tell you what to do.

Next . . .

Stop Over-Explaining and Apologizing

We need to scale back our responses, keeping only to whether we are giving a yes or a no and a general reason as to why. Stop offering so much back story. (Oh, am I ever the queen of this!) The other person does not need to know all the assorted details.

Somehow, we think that piling them on justifies our answer of no. Simply tell them the general reason why and that you must politely decline. No other explanation or apology needed.

Here is a beneficial mantra to memorize . . .

Don't Answer in a Heartbeat. Do a Heart Check.

We often give our answers in a heartbeat. A better practice is to pause and pray, discerning whether your answer should be yes or no; checking your heart to make sure you're not just saying yes in order to be liked and approved of. Don't answer in a heartbeat. Instead, take at least twenty-four hours to ruminate, asking God for his peace. Once you feel you've gotten clear direction, then give your reply. If the person doing the asking simply insists on an answer right then, then tell them the answer will have to be no.

Okay. Here comes one I have to repeatedly remind my own brain of . . .

Stop Making Their Feelings Your Responsibility

Just when did we become solely responsible for the happiness of all those in our lives? An honest look at my life a few years ago taught me that I had made the feelings of others my responsibility. I just couldn't stand to see a family member disappointed, a friend stressed out, or a coworker upset. So I would spring into action, doing or saying things in order to lift their spirits or solve their problems. The feelings of others are not your responsibility. Allow God to work in their lives rather than rushing in to save the day, turning their frown upside down. It's not your job. It is his.

Attempting to be everything to everybody is completely taxing. It saps our mental strength and can wear us out physically. Is signing up to become a drained disciple—trying to meet the needs of everybody at every turn and being solely responsible for their feelings—the life God wants for us? Is this what it means to be servants of Christ? Or, is it ever okay to put yourself first?

Okay, okay. I know this concept stirs up some controversy. But let me explain what I mean by it.

Suit Yourself (For Once!)

Recently I've started making it a habit to listen to some podcasts on my morning walk, when making dinner in the late afternoon, or in the evening when folding laundry before going to bed. My library of favorite podcasts is all over the map. Besides ones designed for spiritual growth, I subscribe to ones on home decorating, current events, history, productivity, and creativity. When I listen, sometimes it is to grow in my walk with the Lord. Other times it's just to be totally entertained.

Recently, after seeing a recommendation online, I decided to listen to a podcast I'd not heard of before. The topic was on self-care. I thought I was going to get some new tips on taking care of myself physically, spiritually, and mentally so I could be at my best—available to minister to others without sacrificing my health. Oh boy, was I ever wrong.

Instead, I heard the concept of self-care trashed and painted as unscriptural. It was completely mystifying from the get-go! The host spoke more of trips to the salon for a fresh mani-pedi, or shopping outings to buy a new item of clothing, than they did about taking time to rest, reflect, and refresh, before venturing back into our lives as women, wives, mothers, and friends. Self-care was wrongly defined as frivolous attention to our hair, makeup, and clothing.

I grew so very frustrated as I listened to the back-and-forth banter of the critical host and her on-air cohort. And, I put myself in the minds of some moms I knew who are in the place I was years ago—emotionally exhausted and physically depleted while caring for young children. The voices emitting from my device seemed to give no room for such a fatigued mom to take a break.

Their solution? If only she trusted Christ more. Prayed more. Believed more. Then she would be able to carry out her many duties in the home, single-handedly handling her small children, and running the entire house by herself.

Although I did not suffer from severe postpartum depression, I have a few friends who did. I shuddered as I thought about what they might think if they had listened to the chastisement that was being broadcast as I stood in my kitchen chopping vegetables for a pot of turkey chili.

So, let me first define what *I* mean by self-care. I'm not speaking of shopping trips and painting your nails a bright shade of fuchsia. (Although I see absolutely nothing wrong with doing either of those things. But make my polish pale peach, not bright fuchsia. It goes so much better with my fair skin tone.) I am talking about pulling away from your responsibilities for an hour—or maybe even a day—or two in order to physically rest, mentally realign your mind, and spiritually connect with God.

Our responsibilities in life, work, church, and community swirl all about us, combining to make the perfect concoction for collapse. We modern-day women are not the first to suffer from such problems. Look at the following passage from the Gospel of Mark, where Jesus and his disciples are dealing with their own dilemma of dizziness. We pick up the story in chapter six.

It is here that we see Jesus interacting with his closest followers. This scene is sandwiched between the time he heard that his cousin, John the Baptist, had been beheaded by King Herod and his feeding five thousand people on a hillside with only five loaves of bread and two fish.

Our Savior's life certainly was full of activities and relationships. There were times of joy and news of sadness. But in the middle of it all we read these words in Mark 6:31, here in the Amplified Version:

> He said to them, "Come away by yourselves to a secluded place and rest a little while"—for there were many [people who were continually] coming and going, and they could not even find time to eat.

Can you relate? People continually coming and going, many of them needing something from you? Your schedule so packed that you can barely find time to sit down for a snack? I don't know about you, but that sounds like a pretty accurate description of my current week. So, what does Jesus suggest as the remedy?

He gives us a magnificent invitation. Read it again. Slowly this time . . . *"Come away by yourselves to a secluded place and rest a little while."*

Oh, so he's telling me to have a pedicure? Buy a new handbag? Nope. He's urging us to do something so much superior.

No doubt you've likely heard of the "five Ws and one H." These are questions to ponder whenever you are gathering basic information, such as for a news report or police investigation. The letters stand for *who, what, when, where, why,* and *how.*

Posed as questions, the answers to the five Ws and one H provide a formula for amassing the complete story of a subject. Let's break down this verse—investigative reporting-style—to see if we can locate the answers to these six questions. (We are going to take them in the order they appear in the verse rather than the traditional sequence.)

First up, "What?" What is Christ inviting us to do?

Come Away . . .

The Greek word from which we get the English word *come* means "to come hither." Now if that old-fashioned word *hither* throws you, its simple definition is "to or toward." When combined with the word translated into English as *away*, it has a variety of meanings, including "after, down from (as in 'to a lower place'), face to face, in the presence of, and privately."

Alright. Our second W is . . .

Who? Who is supposed to come away?

We find the answer in this phrase:

. . . By Yourselves . . .

The Greek practically matches the English here. It means "you, all alone, to the exclusion of others." But another shade of the meaning is revealed when—are you ready?—I just love this rendering . . . *Prompted or influenced by another but of one's own accord.*

Well, that makes it pretty clear that Jesus is doing the calling and that we won't be towing any friends along for this little excursion.

Let's look at the third W.

Where? What is our destination?

. . . To a Secluded Place . . .

The word *place* does mean "location, region, or seat." However, it also can be used to signify an opportunity. Together the words *place* and *secluded* describe a deserted, unpopulated place where quiet and a lack of disturbance are needed.

And to make the picture even clearer, here is the fourth W.

Why? Why do all of this? So that you can . . .

. . . Rest a Little While.

This phrase is best transliterated as: to take a break from your labor, to give oneself quiet, to calmly and patiently rest, and take ease for a brief and short time.

The only thing missing from this verse seems to be the *when* and the *how*. But maybe not. We can discern the when by looking back at the first phrase, *Come away*. The Greek connotation doesn't just mean come. It is an imperative statement and carries with it the force of an interjection. So, it isn't merely stating "Come," but *"Come now!"* It is to be immediate and without haste.

But what about perhaps the most important part—how?

God created each of us so uniquely different from one another. And just as no two of us are exactly alike, there is no slick, one-size-fits-all way to come to Jesus to get the rest he's promised you. In fact, beware of those who would give you a formula—one exclusive path you must take in order to be renewed.

Let's not go beyond what is written in this verse. We must free up a chunk of time to take a break from our labor so we can get away—all alone—to a secluded, unpopulated place where we won't be disturbed, so we may quiet ourselves, seek Jesus privately, lowering ourselves before him, face-to-face, and take a break from our labor. This is an opportunity, as it states in the Greek. And we do it because we are prompted or influenced by another (the Lord), but we come on our own accord. We can't be forced. We must willingly choose.

And when should we do it? As soon as absolutely possible.

How to Stop the Siphoning of Your Soul

I flung myself on the couch, completely exhausted both mentally and physically. My observant and concerned husband offered to take our three small children for an overnight stay at his parents' house to give me some relief, and I jumped at the chance. After all, my schedule was full of taxing duties—running a busy household, caring for a baby and toddler, and also attempting to homeschool a kindergartner (and doing a rather poor job of it, I might add).

I surmised that my problem was busyness. I'd said yes to too many requests and I needed a little break, that's all. But a thirty-six hour stretch of napping and relaxing did not resolve my dilemma. It only made me dread even more when my family would return home, and I'd have to jump back into life, running at breakneck speed.

This wasn't the only time in my life when I experienced such anxiety. As a college student, while taking classes and being heavily involved in student government and other extracurricular activities, I grappled to keep up with everything. I was also my dorm floor's resident assistant, which meant I spent lots of time helping others whether it was letting them in their room when they forgot their key or listening to them when they'd experienced a breakup or loss. As a result, I frequently reached a point where I felt overwhelmed and wanted to run away.

Once I was out of school and pursuing a career, the same feelings of weariness overtook me sometimes, although the circumstances causing them were different.

The truth is, whether chasing a career or chasing the kiddos, caring for a home or for elderly parents, the various roles we have come with responsibilities—responsibilities that can often outpace us, causing us to play a perpetual game of catch-up.

These obligations can siphon the very life from our souls. And the siphoning of our souls is a hard process to stop. However, Psalm 62:5 gives a prescription for our weary souls: "Rest in God alone, my soul, for my hope comes from him" (CSB).

The original Hebrew word here for *rest* means "to grow silent or still." This phrase indicates progression. Our souls sometimes enter a state of unrest and must be quieted. The definition of *soul* here means "a living being, life, self or person." In Hebrew, the soul referred to the seat of a person's passions, appetites, and emotions. It is their very inner being.

The writer of Psalm 62:5 tells us how to remedy our worn-out souls: "Rest in God alone." The word *alone* has an insightful Hebrew meaning here: "in stark contrast to any other ideas; the only solution that works; the real one rather than a counterfeit."

So, when our souls are siphoned due to the draining duties of our roles, or our overcommitment due to people pleasing, we have a guaranteed remedy. And it isn't a nap or a break from our responsibilities—though those things can play a part. The cure is God, who alone can soothe and satisfy our souls. But how?

When we read, study, and even memorize his Word—not as a slick solution we slap on our weariness by checking off certain actions on a list—we make an effort to weave into our souls the life-giving truths we encounter, developing a closer relationship with Jesus as we do.

It also happens when we communicate with him in prayer. More than a quick shopping list of "give-mes" and "bless-thems," but a deep, concentrated time of pouring out our hearts to him. This is how we find rest for our souls—sacred rest only God can provide.

We ignore our souls at our own peril. We try to medicate them with counterfeit means. But they can find true rest only in God and God alone.

Take a rest from your busyness that is a direct result of your people pleasing. Take a break from so much *doing*; switch your plan to *being* with him instead.

It's Your Call

If I were a betting woman, I'd wager that when it comes to thinking of yourself first, your sweet, always-accommodating self has more baggage than carousel three at Chicago's O'Hare airport. We find it foreign. Assume it is wrong. We have both a mixed and messed-up view of the whole idea. But—even though it is a cliché example—the concept is correct: you must first put on your own oxygen mask before attempting to assist others.

Although it has felt as awkward to me as trying to stay in the lines while coloring a butterfly wing in a *Wonders of Nature Coloring Book* with my nondominant hand, I have adopted some practices to help create breathing space for my soul and prevent others from demanding my instant attention. I've realized these measures are not unkind. They are helpful. Not only to me, but to others. I try to keep in mind that I am teaching the people in my life how they are allowed to treat me.

I now regularly put "away messages" on my email account, letting others know when I have a busy week and will not be able to read and answer their email right away. I also give them a date when I will resume correspondence.

I whittled down my personal Facebook account to family members and coworkers, since I only use Facebook to help plan extended family get togethers (such as deciding who is to bring the sweet potato casserole) or to communicate with coworkers on some of the various teams I'm a member of. This didn't go over well with some people in my life. They found it unthinkable that someone would "unfriend" them. And since many of them spend great deals of time clicking and swiping their way around this social media platform and think the more "friends" they have the better, they can't understand why everyone doesn't feel this way about Facebook.

To soften the blow, before starting to narrow down my list, I politely explained in an announcement message that I only used my account for work and family matters. I invited people to hang out with me over on Instagram, the social media platform I love most. I now have only seventy-four Facebook friends, fifty of whom are coworkers. This shorter list prevents my mind from becoming cluttered with tons of useless info, such as what someone I went to church with ten years ago had for lunch. It has also freed up time I can spend as I wish because I no longer feel the pull to hop on for "a few minutes" that always turned into thirty or more.

I have also begun a no-apologies "soul rest budget." I'm able to use this time on a fantastic deal for a bed-and-breakfast room where I can go for an overnight. While there, I can do absolutely nothing but rest, read my Bible, and relax by doing an activity I enjoy, whether it is watching an old movie or writing a letter to a new friend. I can spend smaller amounts of money on items such as a new prayer journal, a Bible study book, an essential oil blend for my diffuser, or—most recently—noise-cancelling headphones for those occasions when I need some peace and quiet. (Although one of my sons also wants to use them to work out to his Beatles music blaring full blast!)

Building margin and rest into your life is possible, even for those of you who have little ones in the house. For years I traded childcare with a friend or got away while the kiddos were spending a little time with their grandparents. Getting creative can help you carve out time to rejuvenate. But it has to be *your* call. *Yours* to decide. *Your* responsibility for your own health in body, soul, and spirit. No other human will do it for you.

It is also God's call, in a way. It is his call to you to come away and find yourself refreshed. Don't worry about what others might say. You only need to please God, not them. Former first lady Eleanor Roosevelt was correct in her assertion when she said, "Do what you feel in your heart will be right, for you'll be criticized anyway."[5]

Will you be bold enough to pray this prayer in earnest, asking God to impart courage to your heart so you may answer his call to come away? Read it with your eyes. Pray it with your heart. Then, follow through and make the rest of your body seek the true rest that only Jesus himself can give.

> *Father, forgive me for ignoring your command to come away with you for a while. I get so busy caring for and accommodating others that I neglect spending unhurried time just sitting at your feet and soaking in your Word. Please help me arrange my circumstances so that I might spend uninterrupted time alone with you soon. May I drink deep of your lavish love and receive the calm and comfort I crave that only comes from you. In Jesus's name. Amen.*

Chapter 8

The Juggle Is Real

Spotted on a coffee mug:
"I am a recovering people pleaser. Is that all
right with you?"

So teach us to number our days,
That we may cultivate and bring to You a
heart of wisdom.
—PSALM 90:12 AMP

How do you keep a schedule? Do you opt for a digital version on your phone, clicking and swiping to enter your appointments and setting reminders for your tasks? Or, are you more of a paper gal, preferring to scrawl out your schedule by putting pen to paper the old-fashioned way? Due to my ministry job at which I work remotely, I have to keep at least my work appointments digitally. This way coworkers can invite me to important meetings I have over Zoom. However, if the choice were mine, I would opt for a spiral-bound planner every time.

I geek out over purchasing calendars and planners. I scour

office supply stores or Etsy shops on the internet each year to find just the perfect one. And the more whimsical and colorful the better. I want a cute font style for the letters prancing across the pages, showcasing for me the medical appointments, home tasks, and work dates I must remember. And, if the cover comes in the perfect shade of salmon pink, robin's egg blue, or lovely buttercup yellow, it makes my heart sing. Won't it look delightful perching on top of my desk, nestled up next to my favorite oversized coffee mug? (Excuse me please while I go snap a pic for Instagram.)

Since I like to think of my year in terms of an academic year—going from August through the following July—those planners are the type I select. And so, each summer, during the final weeks of July, I secure a new planner for the coming academic year, grab my erasable colored pens, and commence making my entries.

These colored pens make it not only look adorable but allow it to be functional as well. I record due dates in blue. For personal time I use purple. I jot down promotions for my blog or social media in pink. Family commitments in green. When I'm done, I spy a lovely rainbow of responsibilities scrawled out upon the pages of this treasured tool.

The only trouble? There's typically not a lot of white space remaining. You see, I have this recurring and harmful habit. Maybe you do too. Because I try to be accommodating and helpful—and also have such a hard time saying no—I easily fall into the pattern of letting others dictate my to-do list, causing quite the overcrowding on my calendar.

I will say that I've gotten better at this over the years. There was a time early on—fresh out of college and newly married—that just looking at my to-do list often made me hyperventilate. That isn't the case anymore. But still. It sneaks up on me slowly.

About every three years, like clockwork, I feel my plate getting way too heavy with all the responsibilities I have placed on it. (Or more accurately, from all the responsibilities I've let others place on my plate without my pushing back!) And so, when I notice I'm once again spread way too thin, I have to face the multitasking music and realize something's got to give.

Sisters, twenty-four hours is all you get. It's all I get. All your most productive friend or least efficient relative gets. All of us have tasks and responsibilities to juggle, brought to us courtesy of our homes, families, jobs, and roles. It seems, however, that all of us don't seek to mesh them in the same way. There are those who are masterful at navigating the tension between their relationships and their responsibilities. Some of the rest of us though? Nah! We stink at this task. I will be the first one to raise my hand and admit it.

After struggling in this area for a couple of decades, I realized the drain it was putting on me. My desire to be known as supportive and helpful was choking out my desire for my days to be manageable and my time to be spent wisely. As a result, my soul was suffering. I love how Lysa TerKeurst puts it in her book *The Best Yes: Making Wise Decisions in the Midst of Endless Demands*. She rightly recognizes the progression.

> The decisions we make dictate the schedules we keep. The schedules we keep determine the lives we live. The lives we live determine how we spend our souls. So, this isn't just about finding time. This is about honoring God with the time we have.[1]

When we allow other people to determine the schedule we keep, we fail to honor God with the time that we have. And our souls are showing it—big time.

So, how do we make sure that our calendars don't become so crowded—using our most colorfully coordinated gel pens—that the items God wishes for us to place there get displaced? It's time we learned to navigate the tension between our people and our punch lists.

Your People and Your Punch List

Each of us has two constant realities vying for attention in our lives: we have people and we have a punch list. But for all of us, these two components are distinctive and the way they combine is unique.

There's the millennial working woman living in a contemporary high-rise apartment in the inner city. She has a nine-to-five dress-up-for-work job, and relationships with coworkers, parents, siblings, and friends. She uses public transit. She volunteers at a local women's shelter on the weekends. Her life is full. Her schedule can get crazy.

Yet another woman may live the life of a full-time wife and mom, wrestling with responsibilities while rustling up dinner for her family of five. She has a baby. And a few young children. And loads of laundry surrounding piles of dishes next to stacks of bills—all of them calling her name. Although most of her time is spent within her four walls, she too feels the tug between her people and her punch list. Her life is full. Her schedule can get crazy.

Just across town from her lives an empty nester. After raising a couple kids, she's down to cooking meals for two. She has a part-time job and aging parents who need her assistance. And now some cherub-faced grandchildren have joyfully entered the scene. Although she thought this empty-nest stage would bring her more time for herself, she was wrong. Her life is full. Her schedule can get crazy.

No matter our season in life—or the various roles in which

we now star—we all have the tendency to let our schedules get cluttered and crazy as we make daily decisions that will affect both our humans and our duties. What we often don't recognize is how the two are closely tangled together. How do we make time for the most important people in our lives while still checking off the boxes on our to-do list? Often, we grant a permission slip to people who should be playing a minor role in our lives, elevating them to the position of executive director and producer. Remember, if you aren't deliberate to prioritize your time, scads of others are out there happy to fill it for you.

So, let's change this, okay? We're going to begin by detecting those in our lives who seem to successfully tend to their tasks without forgetting their folks. There are a few women who jump instantly to mind. They have their people. They have punch lists too. But what they also have is a knack for managing them both without coming unglued.

I remember marveling over how well a friend of mine from a former town seemed to be handling a life that nearly mirrored mine. We were both young married moms with three children each. We were involved in church and community activities and, at that time. were both homeschooling our oldest child. Yet it greatly puzzled me how she seemed so calm and confident in carrying out her tasks and I seemed to incessantly be a day late and a dollar short, frazzled from the overcommitment that resulted from being a people pleaser. And so, I decided to investigate vigilantly how she conducted herself, seeing if I could get her to spill her secrets.

One fall morning, I piled my dear dependents in our old, but trusty, blue minivan and headed downstate to visit with her and her children. Even though we didn't have much planned—besides sipping hot tea while the kids played—I looked forward to the adult human interaction.

I always adored being at this friend's house. A quaint, red brick ranch dwelling, her decor was warm and inviting, perfectly mimicking her personality. We arrived about 9:30 and I sprung the kiddos out of their car seats, grabbed the diaper bag, and headed up her walkway.

After greetings and hugs, we made sure the kids were settled in with their toys and we sat at her kitchen table to catch up on life. As I sipped my orange spiced tea, munching on a delicious muffin she had made for us as a snack that day, I heard her phone ring.

I stopped what I was saying mid-sentence, fully expecting her to grab her phone and answer it. At least that's what I'd made a practice to do in my life. The phone rang, you answered it. So, what surprised me was that she just let it keep ringing and roll over to voicemail. The potential interruption in our conversation didn't seem to faze her at all, nor did she seem curious about who might have been on the other end of that call. In fact, the sound was turned down so she couldn't even hear who was leaving the message.

Finally, my curiosity wouldn't let me keep my lips zipped any longer. And so, I blurted out, "Why didn't you grab that call? I mean, we could've kept visiting once you'd answered it and were finished talking."

She sweetly smiled and, without even having to think about it, gave her answer. "You and I rarely get to spend time together. Whoever was on that phone can wait. Besides, if it were an emergency, they would call right back. But since they just left a message, it must not be something crucial. I will listen to it tonight after supper." Then she nonchalantly sipped her tea and jumped right back into our conversation.

"You mean you won't listen to that message until eight hours or so from now?" I incredulously inquired. "Well," she replied, "I will check to see who it was that called. If it's someone in my family, I'll retrieve the voice mail and then call them back. But for the rest of them, I don't even listen to and return messages until after dinner is done and cleaned up."

I sat there dumbfounded. I guess it never really occurred to me that (a) I don't have to answer the phone the moment it rings, and (b) I didn't have to listen to messages the instant I had a free moment in my day. I think I'd fallen into that habit partly due to my curiosity as to who was calling, and also because I felt it was expected of me. If someone made a comment about my not answering when they rang or about it taking me a while to return their call, I didn't like it. I thought it meant they were subtly implying that either I didn't care about them or I wasn't organized enough to return calls in a timely fashion. But if my friend got a comment like that, it wouldn't ruffle her feathers at all. Because she had something I seemed to lack when it came to juggling my people and tasks.

She had a plan.

The rest of our conversation that morning turned to her plan for managing people and limiting the expectations they put on her. What you need to know is that my friend is not at all a forceful or dominant personality. She's much more laid back. A quiet, unassuming soul. She doesn't exude even a hint of bossiness. But she is fantastic at placing boundaries in her life and coming up with a blueprint for what her day looks like.

I soaked in her every word as she talked about how she never answers the phone during the time she is caring for her children, including homeschooling her oldest who was in the first grade. She determined it just distracted her too much. In fact, she had a few friends in her life who seemed to have oodles of time on their hands. They constantly called to chitchat. As much as she loved these friends, she knew that meeting their expectations of daily discussions wasn't something that interested her. It would keep her from spending time with her kids. It would slow her down and prevent her from accomplishing her obligations around the house. And she wasn't about to let it cut in on her instruction time with her first grader. It was such a novel idea to me that she had close friends—with whom she was in good standing—but she did not let them trump her time with her family or her home responsibilities.

From there our conversation turned to menu planning and grocery shopping. I learned about how she cooked meals ahead, so she wasn't secured to the stove all day. And I discovered how she carved out time to spend with her parents, not to mention her husband, both of whom were high up on her list of folks with whom she needed to connect weekly.

And then I thought back to the many times I had called her during the day, and she didn't pick up. It happened frequently. Then just as she claimed, she would, like clockwork, call me back after supper. And I had to admit, it never had bothered me. She was always cheerful and appeared glad to talk to me when we both had time to do so. I didn't feel put off or slighted in the least. Our friendship was thriving even though she had put some clear and consistent boundaries in place.

After that encounter, I drove home with hope in my heart—and, more importantly, a strategy in my brain—for untangling the relationships-over-responsibilities quandary I was ensnared in. I determined to adopt the same practice in my life. It didn't come easy at all, since the ringing of the phone always seemed to draw me like a chicken strip to honey mustard. Up until then, I rarely ever let a ring roll over to voicemail. But I got myself into a nice little routine. Let the phone ring. Let the caller leave a voicemail. Call them back that evening. Easy peasy.

I stuck to the strategy; slapped my own hand when I was tempted to respond to a ring. Soon, I began to get less calls during the day. True to the old advice, "You teach people how to treat you" rule, friends (and even some chatty relatives) soon knew I was no longer going to sprint to the phone every time I heard it go off.

Her impromptu life lesson to me that day—on managing both your time and your people—sent me off on a mission. I was tired of living my life at the mercy of others. Sick of letting them talk or guilt me into tasks. And I no longer wanted to have barely any white space on my upcoming calendar—or margin in my current day—for simply doing something I found enjoyable.

In fact, it occurred to me that I had not engaged in a hobby in almost a decade. I was too busy being a wife, mom, church member, community worker, neighbor, and family member, to do anything for just pure pleasure.

This on-purpose friend was a striking example of someone who manages their time wisely without neglecting their relationships. She did not allow people to dictate how she used her time, but she still maintained thriving relationships. I learned so much from her.

But the lessons don't stop with our productive and purposeful friends. We can acquire much wisdom from the life of Jesus. Although fully God, he walked the earth as a man. How he conducted himself while dwelling on our spinning orb can also demonstrate for us how to love and serve people without neglecting our work.

A Look at the Lord

When Jesus walked the dusty roads and fields of the Holy Land, he had just as much time as we do: twenty-four hours a day. One-hundred and sixty-eight hours a week. And fifty-two weeks each year. According to the New Testament accounts, he never seemed to be in a hurry. However, he was the Son of God on a very big mission. His life was saturated with people. He had family. Friends. Work, worship, and rest. What can we learn from him about how we are to live our lives, not only successfully, but in a manner that pleases God?

The Gospels show that connecting with his Father was of utmost importance to Christ. He spent time praying and studying the Scriptures, often during situations of concentrated ministry. He consulted God before he selected his ministry team—the twelve disciples. He prayed when carrying out assignments of his mission, including the feeding of five thousand famished people one afternoon. We observe the Lord praying as he primed for a trying time—whether in the throes of a crisis or before his arrest in the Garden of Gethsemane. He also withdrew to pray when ministry threatened to overwhelm him.

Spending time communing with God to revitalize himself was elevated to the top of his priority list—perhaps even written in bright, red permanent ink. He had hidden God's Word in his heart. Even Satan coming against him in the wilderness didn't stand a chance. Jesus reflexively quoted Scripture from memory to combat the devil and his ploys.

Is being in the presence of God—connecting through prayer and Bible study—of paramount significance to you? Does your schedule prove it? Or, are you content to check off a few quick prayer requests and do a little devo dance before busting into your day? Like waving to a high school friend in the hallway before first period, do you say, "Hey!" to Jesus in the morning but then totally ignore him the rest of the day? I hate to admit that somedays my answer to this last question would be a big, fat yes. *Sigh*.

Jesus had a packed agenda while on earth, peppered with both people and purpose:

- At times his ministry involved preaching the good news to multitudes. He fed a hungry crowd or healed a woman who reached out to touch his robe amid a throng of others (Matthew 5:1–7:29; Matthew 14:13–21; Mark 5:24–35).
- He had family members that included not only his parents

but his four half-brothers—James, Joseph, Judas, and Simon—and his cousin John the Baptist (Matthew 13:55; Luke 1:36).

- He poured into a group of seventy-two, training them before they embarked on a harvest mission for the kingdom (Luke 10:1–3).
- A great majority of the time, he hung out with the twelve disciples, showing them up close and personal, by his words and actions, how to live by example (Matthew 10:1–5; Mark 10:32–34).
- And the Lord even had an inner circle of those who were closest to him: Peter, James, and John (Matthew 17:1–3; Mark 14:32–34; Luke 8:51–52).

Strangers cheered him. Religious leaders criticized him. Some even plotted to take his life.

While Jesus had numerous people in his life, he also had a plan. Through it all, he never let the people deter him from his main assignment.

The Spirit of the Lord is on me, because he has anointed me to proclaim good news to the poor. He has sent me to proclaim freedom for the prisoners and recovery of sight for the blind, to set the oppressed free, to proclaim the year of the Lord's favor. (Luke 4:18–19)

It fascinates me how Jesus stayed true to his mission but knew how to manage his interactions with people. He didn't let the crowds overcome him. He sometimes singled out individuals such as the woman at the well (John 4:1–26), the woman with the issue of blood (Mark 5:24–35), and the rich young ruler (Luke 18:18–23). He remained consistent in his calling and yet confident in his human interactions, knowing when to pour into others and when to withdraw to rest.

Speaking of rest, Jesus was serious about the Sabbath, although he was not legalistic. He recognized our need to follow the pattern shown in creation of laboring six days and resting on the seventh. But he did take into account emergencies that might occur on the Sabbath day. He avowed that the Sabbath was made for man, not the other way around. So, if an animal needed rescuing, or an individual needed healing, he altered his normal routine and tended to them on the day of rest.

He would not be categorized as idle or lazy. He did his work with gusto and efficiency. Just take a highlighter sometime and go through the Gospel of Mark, picking out every time you see the word *immediately*. Jesus was an on-purpose person. He wasn't a time waster. He was the epitome of the adage, "work smarter, not harder." We don't see him allowing the expectations and wishes of others to deter him from his mission or make him emotionally exhausted. He toggled between work, people, and rest success-fully, and in a way that pleased God.

If we want to learn to be successful with both relating to our people and setting our own schedules, we first need to tackle a topic that Jesus lived out. Scads of blog posts have been written about it; scores of sermons preached about it. But do we really understand what it means to live by it?

I'm talking about priorities.

Priority Treatment

Nearly a decade after my encounter with my wise friend—who did not allow her schedule to be dictated by everyone else in her life—I started a blog. Actually, I began it at her urging. God had taught me so much about juggling my people and my tasks;

pleasing him and serving them while refusing to be overrun with their assignments for me.

I wanted the focus of my blog to be on helping other people make strides in this area as well. And so, I came up with a tagline: *Live Your Priorities. Love Your Life.*

I'd made an observation that the women who most seemed to love their lives—who were able to balance hard work with great enjoyment of their families and even some leisure activities—were the ones who truly lived their priorities. And so, in each blog entry, I tried to provide creative solutions and doable ideas for women to tend to the priorities in their lives, whether it was their relationships with God and the members of their family or wise time management so that they could accomplish the tasks God had called them to do.

Before long, I ascertained that what was most needed in this area was advice on how to actually live your priorities, being proactive rather than reactive. Women needed to be empowered to be the "Decider-in-Chief" of their own agenda, making sure that what actually made it onto the calendar page or phone app was a direct order from God, rather than simply a result of trying to make someone else happy.

When asked our priorities, most of us would put God first, our close family members second, followed by work, friends, and so on down the list. However, often the reality of our behavior depicts quite a different scenario.

Years earlier, I had been challenged in the area of priorities because I'd finally conceded mine were completely out of whack. If you were to have asked me what my priorities were, I would have responded that they were these, in the following order:

1. God
2. My husband
3. My children

4. Other extended family members
5. My job (I was only working part time at a home business.)
6. My responsibilities as a church member
7. My close friends
8. My neighbors and other, not-so-close friends
9. My responsibilities outside of the home
10. Everybody and everything else

The problem became evident when you looked at how I not only planned but executed my days. The reality of my schedule did not at all match up with what I said my priorities were. I was often letting a priority that was high on the list get usurped by something further down the page.

Now, it's a little tricky when thinking about God being the number-one priority. I'm not suggesting this means we spend the greatest amount of time with him each day. We can't study the Bible for eight hours and neglect all the rest of our responsibilities. It's more the thought of, *Do I carve out time to spend time with him daily, making it a priority? Do I devote time daily to learning from God's Word and communicating with him through prayer? Or, do I allow other things to crowd out my time with him?*

It's the same concept with a full-time job outside the home. That may take up the greatest bulk of your day, simply because it has to. But again, it's all about matter of importance. Are you allowing interruptions throughout your workday by people further down your list who keep calling, texting, or needing things from you in some other way?

Here's how it looked when I did my experiment, keeping track not only of how I was spending my time but which people and priorities I was certain to not miss each day and what other ones I simply passed over or ignored.

I was supposed to be attending to something with one of my

children (a priority number three). However, along came a number eight—a not-so-close friend or an acquaintance from church. They either knocked on my door, made my phone vibrate, or sent me an email imploring me to help them put out their fire. Soon their crisis became my crisis, and so what did I do? I placed my child on hold and ran off to save the world.

In order to really scrutinize how often this was happening, I tacked a list of what I said my priorities were on the bulletin board near the desk where I blogged. Then, for about three weeks I watched myself like a hawk, keeping track of how often each day I was spending with my family, my ministry work, my household responsibilities, as well as how often each day I was processing with or helping other people.

I was shocked when, at the end of the three weeks, I tallied my habits. While my home and family did receive the greatest chunk of my time, I was allowing my days to be filled from the outside by assisting people who were not my close friends but whom I had trained by my behavior to come to me for ... well ... just about anything!

I missed many days reading and studying my Bible or spending time in prayer (number-one on my priority list). But I rarely missed a day returning someone's phone call, email, or text (priority numbers four, seven, eight, and ten).

This revealing exercise lit a fire under me that day. I no longer wanted to be at the mercy of others' agendas for my days, at their beck and call each instant. I desired so deeply for the way I spent my time to align with what I purported my priorities to be.

Over the years, I have challenged many women at my speaking events to do this very same thing. Craft their list. Watch their behavior. See how it lines up. So often, I received emails a few weeks after the events from these ladies who delivered me their results.

There were a handful for whom the exercise was very confirming; they were essentially spending their time in a way that lined up with what they asserted their priorities to be. But for others, an entirely contrasting scenario emerged. So many admitted that they were allowing priority numbers eight through ten (emphasis on the ten!) to outmaneuver priorities number two through four.

I vividly recall one woman, who was very close to a group of friends who all enjoyed digital scrapbooking. She divulged that she never missed scrapbooking sessions each week but often neglected focused time with her husband and spent merely a flicker of time reading and studying the Bible. Because her hobby was tied to her buddies, she never abandoned it.

If we purpose to live by our priorities, it is going to alter our schedules. Rather than just allowing the infiltration of tasks that result from the many asks we receive—or from our own misguided guilt and lack of planning—we can intentionally craft our calendars in a way that lines up with both what and who are of greatest importance in our lives. Getting there might not be fun, but it will be effective, and you will feel the satisfaction of having your priorities in line!

Access Denied

I swiped open my phone and brought up the app to the bank where my husband and I have our money stashed. Since I want to have the greatest amount of security on that account, I never save my username or password, but enter it in manually each time I need to check my bank account. I know it seems like a hassle, but my paranoia outshines the inconvenience, making me feel a little more secure.

That morning, however, no matter how many times I tapped out my username and password, the same bright red block letters kept dancing across my screen "ACCESS DENIED." What in the world? I could not figure out what was going on. Every few days or so, I would check both of our savings and checking accounts, making sure nothing wonky was happening or any charges appeared that I hadn't authorized. (Ahem . . . like a UFC fight pass for $59.99 that my son bought so he and his pizza-eating buddies could watch the matches one night!)

Finally, it occurred to me what was wrong. I was entering in a username and password all right. However, it was not the one to our bank account. It was the one to the cash app I use to collect money from my children when they owe me for something. (And it came in quite handy when I discovered that unauthorized UFC Fight Pass charge.)

For many of us, it is as if the username and password to our schedules have been broadcast publicly, granting unauthorized usage to the people in our lives. They keep hacking their way into our account and filling our time. Of course, it's not entirely their fault. We are allowing them to do it. Still, it's time we changed the login info and started denying them access.

Here are some measures to put in place that will help us begin to successfully juggle our responsibilities and relationships in a way that pleases God without maxing us out.

Start with Your Nonnegotiables

Take your blank calendar—whether the digital or paper variety—and place on it any nonnegotiables in your life. These are the things that cannot be changed. Fill in blocks of time, including work hours, time caring for kids or other relatives, household duties, and church commitments.

Next, Leave Some White Space

This is next in importance after your nonnegotiables because it is crucial to your mental health. Block out some white space for taking a break, enjoying a hobby, or simply doing nothing. It doesn't have to be a lot.

There are seasons in life when we don't have a great deal of white space. When I was a full-time mom of two small children and a nursing infant, with a husband working tons of overtime at an automobile factory, I only got about an hour by myself each week, but boy, was that hour needed! Care about your own mental health enough to fight for some white space in your week. If you can afford the luxury, give yourself thirty minutes per day of completely unscheduled time. This is not the only time you will take for yourself, but it can be used (as necessary) to help someone else who truly requires your assistance.

Then, Compose Your Own Rules of Thumb

Come up with specific rules that you will stick to as closely as you can. Maybe you will not return voicemails and messages until the evening. One person I know has rules for her interactions with others. She responds to Facebook comments on Tuesdays and private messages in Instagram on Thursdays, answers emails on Mondays and Wednesdays, and then walks away from her email and social media accounts Friday through Sunday. As for text messages and voicemails, she only responds to urgent ones as they come in and takes a half hour each night to respond to the others. If she doesn't get to it that evening, it rolls over until the next evening. People in her life know these guidelines so they aren't expecting an immediate reply and they learn to adapt to her practices.

Okay, the following one has freed me a time or two. It is . . .

Announce Instead of Apologizing

It does you no good to come up with some parameters and procedures, and then fall all over yourself apologizing about them to others. Don't apologize; announce. Here is what this looks like:

When you return someone's call, don't begin with, "Hey, I'm so sorry I'm just now getting back to you, but I'm trying not to return voicemails until after supper." Say, "I've just now listened to your voicemail from this morning . . ." and then simply give them your reply. If they make a comment about it taking you a while to respond, don't flinch. *You can do it!* Just declare, "In order to use my time more effectively, I respond to all voicemails at once in the early evening." The. End. Game. Over. No further explaining necessary.

This next one is a fun way to keep yourself on track . . .

Make Yourself a Visual Reminder

Some of us do well to have a visual reminder. Create it either by hand, using card stock and colored pencils or markers, or on your computer. List your priorities in order. You can even start by listing the first one at the top of the page in large font and then add successive priorities in fonts of decreasing size. Having such a reminder on your desk—or better yet, as a screensaver on your phone—can coax you into remembering your priorities as you deal with your people and execute your projects.

Not wanting to go it alone? Then . . .

Enlist the Help of Another Priority-Challenged Friend

No doubt you are not the only one struggling to figure out how to maintain your relationships while also getting life done. Grab a friend who also wants to grow in this area. Text each other when you need support. You could check in with each other once a week to see how things are going. It's helpful to know that you are not alone. Having a companion to provide support and a fresh perspective can help make the journey a little easier.

Here's something we don't often think about . . .

Remind Yourself That This Won't Just Help You but Will Benefit Others in the Long Run

When you begin to be serious about setting a schedule that pleases God and doesn't overwhelm you, you may get pushback from others. Or, you may get hit with a gush of guilt or feel like you are being unkind. When you draw some lines and enact some best practices, remind yourself that not only are you doing this to save your sanity, but that it will also benefit others in the long run. Enabling someone to push or guilt you into something is not helping them out. It is reinforcing their unhealthy behavior. Perhaps they need someone to stand up to them, refusing to be a pushover anymore. It will teach them to respect boundaries and honor another's wishes.

Finally, while attempting to guard your time and your schedule, don't be overly rigid. God may have other plans, so . . .

Be Sensitive to the Holy Spirit's Promptings

Don't take this practice too far. Often overcorrecting can land us in the other ditch. We don't want to be inflexible and unwilling to allow God to interrupt our schedule and divert our attention to something he has planned for us. Be sensitive to those times when the Holy Spirit will tap you on the heart, telling you to switch your plans and alter your schedule. The key is making sure this is a God appointment and not someone pressuring you, interrupting your agenda.

The Priority-Infused Soul

I grabbed the antique sewing basket that had belonged to my Grandma Elsie when she was alive. I swung by the fridge to grab a pineapple kombucha and then sauntered out to sit in a patch of sunshine on the bench at the edge of our front brick walkway. The rushing of the waterfall over the rocks in our small pond nearby was soft and soothing. I settled in for a half hour of doing something that once had been nonexistent in my schedule, but that was now built in daily. What was this new activity?

Doing whatever I wanted to!

This day, it was making some progress on a new embroidery project I bought—a cute bamboo hoop that sported three succulent plants splashed across the cream-colored muslin fabric. My mom had taught me to embroider when I was in elementary school. However, I hadn't picked up a project since college, even though I thoroughly enjoyed doing it. I just never seemed to be able to find—*I mean, make*—the time.

Some days I spent my half hour reading a book I actually *wanted* to read, not just one I needed to peruse for work. Other days I took my iPad out to the back deck and searched for new recipes or decorating ideas on Pinterest. Sometimes I grabbed a comfy throw blanket, set a timer for thirty minutes, and then cuddled up on the couch in front of our fireplace and drifted off for a delightful catnap. Divine!

Now, a half hour carved out of a day to do something I wanted might not seem a big deal. But for me, it was a monumental shift. Before starting to break free from the prison of people pleasing, I rarely had time to breathe, let alone make any real time for myself. Because I was putting out everyone else's fires, saying yes to helping with everyone else's tasks, and offering my assistance whenever I caught wind of a need, I was crowding out any time I could devote to savoring a little bit of leisure.

Do you know what percent of a day a half hour is? Barely 2 percent! To be precise, it is exactly 2.083 percent of your twenty-four hours. That's it! But somehow, this 2-percent breather allows me to punch the reset button on my brain and tackle the rest of my day with enthusiasm.

I would never have begun to make this daily practice happen if I hadn't learned the importance of living a priority-infused life—one that positions me best for work and ministry; one that doesn't overcrowd my schedule or sap my soul by running around trying to be everything to everyone.

All of us have people. Each of us has a punch list. We must recognize what an immense privilege both of these are. We have souls in our lives; souls we can love on and learn from; souls we can serve and be comforted by. And we also have work. For me today, it might be weeding my herb garden, baking a banana cake, or answering a ministry email. I'm so grateful to have both meaningful work and people who mean the world to me.

However, I've also realized that I have a responsibility when it comes to these people and these tasks. I can't just allow my day to be filled by whoever is wanting to direct my time. When I make it my aspiration to get my marching orders from the Lord, I can then move forward in confidence, setting my schedule while also interacting with those he has placed in my life.

It's certainly not a practice that can be cultivated overnight. It takes trial and error. It also most certainly takes guts. Not everyone is going to be jazzed about your new practice of trying to please God while setting your own schedule and determining to whom you will give your time.

A wise mentor once said to me that the more deliberate you want to be with your time, and the greater your desire to please God with your schedule, the more people you must be willing to disappoint. Oh sisters, was she spot-on! I know I've disappointed others; others who were so accustomed to me helping them live life, caring little that it was at the expense of me living my own! I've let others down who'd grown to expect me to persistently lighten their load so they could have some free time. And in the most extreme cases, I stopped letting the bullies push me around and intimidate me into setting my schedule according to their wishes. And the bullies didn't like it one iota. But one thing I know for certain is this . . .

It was, without question, one of the healthiest decisions I've ever made.

Take the time to do the hard work. Get honest before the Lord and allow him to help you clear your schedule. Wipe it sparkling clean. Then place back on it only the tasks and people he is calling you to.

We needn't feel guilty. Jesus didn't spend every waking minute constantly catering to others. He didn't stop to talk with every single soul he met. He had a clear focus, knowing his mission and his ministry; taking care to interact with the people—however many or few—were on God's agenda for him that day. May we seek to do the same; not worrying so much about disappointing others, but caring more that our thoughts, desires, and actions are pleasing to God.

Your people. Your punch list. The juggle is real. Thankfully, so is the help you will get from the Lord. He will empower you to manage the tension between both and then navigate your days with confidence.

Chapter 9

It All Comes Down
to You and Jesus

*If you live for people's acceptance, you will die
from their rejection.*
—RECORDING ARTIST LECRAE

*I love those who love me;
And those who seek me early and diligently
will find me.*
—PROVERBS 8:17 AMP

On September 11, 2001, the most devastating terrorist attack on American soil transpired at three different locations: the World Trade Center in New York City, the Pentagon outside Washington, D.C., and a field in Shanksville, Pennsylvania.

What was considered normal life was temporarily altered. Activities ceased. People were glued to their television sets. Even America's pastime, major league baseball, canceled its games immediately following the attacks. When play did resume, the season was pushed back a few weeks.

Then, on October 30 of that year, game three of the 2001 World Series was held in Yankee Stadium in the Bronx. It was decided that the president at the time, George W. Bush, would throw out the first pitch. It wouldn't be easy, not because he was a fifty-five-year-old man trying to hurl a baseball sixty feet, six inches across home plate, but because he would be wearing a bulletproof vest when he did.

Before tossing out that ceremonial pitch, President Bush got a little advice from the Yankees' captain, the legendary Derek Jeter. The president was planning to throw the ball from a location slightly closer than the actual pitching mound that the players used. However, Jeter suggested he didn't. Not only did he insist that the president needed to throw the ball the entire distance, but that Bush knew the importance of getting it all the way across home plate. And so, to add to the gravity of the feat, before the president left to walk out to the field, Jeter looked at him and gave the Commander in Chief one potent piece of advice, "Don't bounce it or they'll boo you."

The president—now mulling over the thought that his ball might not make it all the way to the catcher without touching the ground—trotted from the dugout to the mound. Then, in the midst of roaring applause and chants of "U-S-A, U-S-A," he reached the top of the mound, greeted the crowd for a moment, and hurled a strike dead center across home plate.

Nobody—Democrat or Republican—was booing him then.

"Boo! Did I Scare Ya?"

We desperately fear the boos of others. It doesn't matter if it's while performing work in our profession or how we raise our kids, we don't want to face the jeers and taunts of the crowd. Unfortunately, this isn't limited to when we actually do fail to perform something correctly. For those of us who are people pleasers, it also applies to being booed by someone when we fail to follow their plans for our life.

I desperately wish I had learned this lesson earlier. I spent decades working hard, hyper-performing, overachieving, being exceedingly helpful, and almost nauseatingly nice just to keep the boos at bay.

My elementary school-aged-self wanted nothing more than to please my teachers. And the playground attendant. And the school secretary. And especially the principal. Gaining their affirmation not only made me feel accomplished. It made me feel secure.

My preteen and teenage-self craved the cheers of my peers. I wanted to be chosen for the team during gym class. Elected to the student council. And if I could only make it onto the ballot for homecoming court, wouldn't that be remarkable? I made a myriad of decisions during that half decade or so of my life, each directly because of what it would do to my reputation in the eyes of my peers.

Adulthood didn't really alter things much. I still spent time performing in order to bring on the "atta girl!" gushes and keep the boos to a bare minimum. I made decisions in my marriage, my mothering, and my ministry, all because I wanted adulation and didn't want to get jeered.

Keeping the crowd from booing is exhausting. And constant. It pecks at our brains and eats away at our souls. When we conduct our lives terrified of the reaction of the crowd, we can't keep our focus on the One whose opinion, love, and acceptance really matters.

At the end of our lives, we aren't going to be graded on how loud the crowds were roaring, cheering us on as we met their expectations. No. It all comes down to you and Jesus. He is the only one sitting in the bleachers. We are performing for an audience of one.

Just Who Is Getting Their Way?

When we've finally reached our boiling point from trying desperately to make everyone else happy, we stomp our feet and declare, "I'm so stinking tired of letting everyone else get their way!" Due to our failure to stand up for ourselves—or to guard our time and mental capacity—we allow others to get their way. We get controlled. Become a "yes woman." We over-serve. We go along to get along. Repeatedly.

However, if we are being completely honest, that is not the totality of the tale. In allowing others' desires for our behavior to be fulfilled, it's not just the pushers, pouters, guilt bombers, and other assorted souls who are the ones who come out on top. There is another beneficiary of our behavior. Oh, I'd venture to guess that you may never have thought of it this way before, so hang with me. There *is* someone else who is getting their own way.

You are.

The self-reflection excursion God has had me on for the past few years has made me face the music. Yes, I let others get their way. However, when I do, in a way I also get mine. I want to be approved of. Appreciated. Liked and adored. And so, when I give in and people-please, in a strange, convoluted way, I am eventually achieving my desired endgame. There is a term in the Bible that is at the core this type of behavior. Two terms, to be exact. And honestly, I think they may surprise you.

From Boos to Bows

"Well," the fellow team mom asked, "can you do it?" I sat in my lawn chair in foul territory near first base, nursing my gas station cup of hot cocoa, trying to craft my response. This woman, who was the mother of another baseball player on my son's travel team, had just laid out a long list of duties that needed to be accomplished for the team's end-of-year party. To top it off, she not only asked if I would spearhead the event, but she wanted to know if we could host it at our home.

I knew she had worded her question asking if I *could* do it, not if I wanted to. Oh, I could do it all right. It is totally in my wheelhouse to organize an event, gather food and decorations, plan games, and host a bang-up party. I planned all the campus social events for my college, for crying out loud. It would be a piece of cake! But the truth was, even though I *could* do it, I so didn't want to.

I was dealing with the tragic news that my sister-in-law—who was also one of my closest friends—was facing a recurrence of her breast cancer. We were told to hold an early Christmas that year in the fall, because she might not be around December 25th. And so, I tried to visit her as often as possible, which meant about four hours on the road each time. Also, we'd recently moved to a new home and were still unpacking boxes. To top it all off, I was working on a new book and I needed to dedicate every spare moment I could to getting it to my editor by the deadline.

Trying to function in the midst of those realities made me want to politely decline. But I knew how much this mom was counting on me. Also, our family was new to this team and—if I'm being entirely truthful—I wanted to show them how clever and capable I was when it came to throwing a successful baseball bash. And so, I obliged. I told her I would be happy to be in charge. So why after answering her didn't I *feel* happy?

People pleasing is often steeped in pride. I probably would not have admitted that years ago. But now I know it to be wholly true. We want to be thought of as competent and capable. We long to keep up a good image. It was my pride that day that wouldn't let me admit that I was not able to handle organizing the year-end get together without overly stressing me out and infringing on my family time. So I took the challenge and planned a fabulous party. Everyone raved about the ballpark-themed food and the clever games. They were pleased, and I—though frazzled—had reached my goal of looking good in the eyes of others, earning their approval. My willingness to be in charge didn't bring me boos. Instead, I was able to take a bow. And, as is often the case, pride brought me praise, but it adversely affected my walk with Jesus.

If we want to dismantle the patterns of people pleasing in our lives, we must sincerely examine our hearts to see if we have a problem with pride. I like to think of it as having "I" trouble. "I" think only about how "I" will look to others when "I" am asked to be in charge, help out, perform a task, do a duty . . . you name it. When "I" say yes, "I" keep my stellar image so "I" continue to be thought well of. It is all about the "I"s.

The subject of pride is scattered in verses throughout the Bible, at least 107 times by my count. It isn't a subject we should gloss over lightly, thinking the verses don't apply to us. It's easy to read the Bible and then apply the Scriptures to someone else we know. But when we do so, we are reading the Bible wrong. Instead, we need to ask ourselves if we see our own behavior staring back at us from its pages.

Now, I'm not talking about pride in the sense that you feel satisfied about an accomplishment. Nor the pride you feel over one of your children or your spouse or your newly organized pantry, complete with your spices in alphabetical order. I am defining pride the way the Bible does.

In the Old Testament, the Hebrew word for the noun *pride* is *ga'own*. It comes from the root word *geeh*, an adjective which means "proud." Both of these terms refer to being "arrogant, lofty, and pompous." One who is prideful is exactly that—full of pride!

Flip, tap, or scroll your way through the book of Proverbs and you will notice the topic of pride addressed several times.

According to Proverbs 11:2, "When pride comes, then comes disgrace, but with humility comes wisdom." When we choose to be prideful, disgrace is not far behind. The Hebrew word for *disgrace* means "reproach, dishonor, and shame." How interesting that when we puff ourselves up with pride, we think we are elevating ourselves in the eyes of others. But the result is the exact opposite. We will reap reproach, dishonor, and shame.

Notice this verse also asserts that with humility comes wisdom. *Chokmah* is the Hebrew word for *wisdom*. It means "skill in war or technical work." It also means "prudence in religious and ethical affairs." When we fight against pride, we usher in wisdom, and wisdom helps us to live a right and righteous life before God.

The book of Proverbs also showcases something else that often goes along with pride. See if you can catch it from reading these next two verses.

> Pride goes before destruction,
> a haughty spirit before a fall. (Proverbs 16:18)

> Before a downfall the heart is haughty,
> but humility comes before honor. (Proverbs 18:12)

What an ominous prediction! When we harbor pride or haughtiness in our hearts, we are in for a fall. And not just a slight one, mind you, but one that leads to destruction.

Recently, the president of our ministry was talking about this very concept in our weekly staff meeting. While delivering a devotion, she talked about pride, keying in on two words: *humiliated* and *humbled*. I loved the description she gave when explaining the difference between these two states of being.

The humble person bows their own knee to be brought low. They do not think of themselves more highly than they ought because they have an accurate assessment of themselves. However, the one who is humiliated staggers from the results of pride. However, they didn't lower themselves to that humble position. Instead, their pride caused them to trip and fall.

Pride trips us up.

Also, it is important to notice what God thinks of the prideful person. This topic is covered in both the Old and New Testaments.

> To fear the LORD is to hate evil;
>> I hate pride and arrogance,
>>> evil behavior and perverse speech. (Proverbs 8:13)

> The LORD Almighty has a day in store
>> for all the proud and lofty,
> for all that is exalted
>> (and they will be humbled). (Isaiah 2:12)

> All of you, clothe yourselves with humility toward one another, because "God opposes the proud but shows favor to the humble." (1 Peter 5:5)

God hates pride and arrogance. Those are some mighty strong sentiments. He has a plan for the proud and lofty, and it isn't a pretty one. They will be brought low. And, he opposes the proud. They are on opposite teams, so to speak. However, he shows favor to the humble.

I'm sure we would all rather not trip and fall before we learn to look to the Lord in humility. Humbling ourselves is a wiser place to start.

James 4:10 echoes this: "Humble yourselves before the Lord,

and he will lift you up." And we also find this notion in Proverbs 29:23: "Pride brings a person low, but the lowly in spirit gain honor."

In doing my own word study on the topic of pride, I checked some cross references that pointed out verses that might not have the word *pride* in them but were related none-the-less. I love the image depicted in Psalm 3:3, which reads,

> But You, O LORD, are a shield for me,
> My glory and the One who lifts up my head. (NKJV)

When we are proud, we do not bow to anyone else but ourselves. We are standing tall, without any posture of humility. But the psalmist says that the Lord lifts up our head. A close friend of mine once made a very startling discovery when she was herself in a place of pride. While spending time reading the Bible one morning, she happened across this verse. Her eyes scanned the words about the Lord lifting up our head. It was then that it hit her like a ton of bricks. She felt as if God was whispering to her heart, *Sweet child. I cannot lift a head that is not bowed.*

Wow. I know! Take a minute to let that one sink in. I'll be here waiting.

You back? Good. Me too. Well, the choice is ours: humble ourselves—bowing our heads and our hearts—or be too proud to be honest with people so we can keep up our accomplished reputations. When we choose the latter, we are in for a slip and fall.

Pride will entice us to overexaggerate our character in order to win friends. It will tempt us to minimize our flaws. It will coax us into doing whatever is necessary to keep up a solid image before others, garnering bows and avoiding the boos. This type of hyper-pride is affiliated with another term in Scripture—*idolatry.*

Whoa. Yes, you read that right. But please don't label me a heretic quite yet. Let me make my case for that audacious statement.

What Is Idolatry?

Most of us have never entertained the notion that we might have a problem with idolatry. I mean, come on! Isn't idolatry behaving like the ancient Israelites did when they melted all their jewelry and artifacts to fashion a golden cow, and then bowed down and worshiped it? Or, maybe certain religions today erect statues and construct altars and then worship before them, in hopes that the gods will treat them favorably. Because I doubt many of us have a precious metal bovine figurine gracing our living room, aren't Scriptures that warn about idolatry irrelevant to us?

At least thirty times in the New Testament we see the subject of idolatry cited. The early church was warned against the adulation of idols and we modern-day believers are still to heed that warning. But just what is an idol? Does it have to be made by human hands, fashioned out of gold, bronze, or silver?

The Greek word that was used for our English word *idol* is the word *eidolon*. Its uncomplicated definition is "an image, whether real or imaginary." Thus, idolatry is the worship of an image, either one crafted by humans or one that is imaginary. It becomes something that is exalted; it takes the place of God.

Okay. By now you are shaking your head and speculating, *But how in the world is people pleasing like idolatry?* Because of this progression: when we people-please, often it is rooted in pride. Our pride makes us behave certain ways in order to maintain our reputation of being capable, competent, or compassionate. And so, we in fact are worshiping an image—our own! We are worshiping the image we are trying desperately to keep up. And sadly, we often strive to perpetuate this image to the point where it becomes more important than our relationship with God.

Nineteenth-century evangelist and publisher Dwight L. Moody observed, "You don't have to go to heathen lands today to find false gods. America is full of them. Whatever you love more than God is your idol."[1]

When we elevate the opinions and expectations of others above all else, we are putting them in the place of God. When we pursue keeping up a certain image at all costs, we exalt our own reputation over our relationship with Christ. Both of these actions kick God out of first place in our lives, swapping him out for someone lesser. And—worst of all—both actions lessen our love for God. Whatever we love more than God is our idol.

We are warned in Psalm 106:36 of such idolatry: "They worshiped their idols, which became a snare to them." There is that word snare again! Remember *moqesh* in the Hebrew? We are tripped up and trapped when we place anything above God, even our own image. However, making sure that God has first place in our thoughts and is directing our actions can be challenging. After all, for so long we have fallen into the pattern of people pleasing. Things are not going to change overnight. But perhaps you are at the point that I was a few years ago: so thoroughly sick of being snared by this detrimental pattern. Allow the Lord to be your confidence and to gently lead you out of the land of people pleasing. King Solomon tells us how this can happen, again using a word we are well familiar with by now.

> Do not be afraid of sudden terror
> or of the ruin of the wicked, when it comes,
> for the LORD *will be your confidence*
> *and will keep your foot from being caught.* (Proverbs
> 3:25–26 ESV, emphasis mine)

We need to check our pride at the door and not allow it to get carried to the extreme of idolatry: spiritual entanglement. The Lord himself can be our confidence, empowering us to care more about his opinion than the opinions of others.

The Focus Factor

Over the years, I've had a number of jobs. I was a dishwasher and waitress in my father's restaurant when I was in my final years of high school. I served as an occasional house cleaner, full-time babysitter, and a part-time sports reporter for a local radio station all before the age of twenty. In college, I was a resident assistant in a dormitory and planned the social life activities for the entire campus. Today, I get paid to write books and Bible studies and speak at church and community events. But if you want to know which of my jobs was my absolute favorite, it was the five years I spent being a substitute teacher in our local school district.

Yep. I loved being a substitute teacher, and I even requested to be placed at the middle school, the building where most substitutes dreaded going. But there wasn't any spit wad shooting, "Kick Me!" sign placing, or other practical-joke-playing on my watch. I loved the kids and they loved me. It probably helped that my husband was a youth pastor who visited the school during lunch hour a few times a week. He'd built up a good rapport with the students and, as a side benefit, I didn't get an ounce of trouble from them.

It wasn't just the kids who made me love this job. I love to be spontaneous and mix things up, so I don't get bored. No matter if it was woodshop or orchestra, gym class or ceramics, every day was different. I didn't even mind when I got to the classroom and there were no assignments left because the teacher had suddenly come down ill that morning. I just improvised.

One of the games I remember playing with the kids involved

a blindfolded student positioned on one side of the room, with me, the teacher, stationed on the other. I would select eight or so students to stand randomly in the classroom between the chosen student and me. The goal was for the blindfolded pupil to make their way to where I stood, listening for my voice giving them directions. The only trouble was that all the other students were free to talk, laugh, and holler—anything they wanted to do to try to distract the blindfolded one. I, on the other hand, was only able to talk in a normal speaking volume.

Often, hilarity ensued. The blindfolded student would get very confused when trying to discern my voice over those of the other classmates. Some savvy students even tried their very best to mimic my voice, completely throwing off the one who was trying to find their way.

While I used this classroom game as an illustration to dialogue about making wise choices in the midst of all that was screaming for their attention, I think it applies so well to the topic we've been discussing for the last eight and a half chapters. We need to lean in and listen discerningly, heeding the voice of God above all the other voices of humans, and noises of the world, that clamor for our attention and seek to fill our schedules. When we become more consistent in doing this, we can learn to walk in confidence and security, owning our choices and deciding for ourselves where and how we will spend our time. When we listen to—and follow—the Lord, confusion lessens, and confidence rises.

I find strength in thinking of some of the people in biblical times who followed God despite the opinions and expectations of others.

- Noah stood strong and forged forward, while everyone else thought he was crazy to build an ark when there wasn't even a rain cloud in sight.

- Joseph didn't give in to the desires of Mrs. Potiphar—perhaps the first desperate housewife!—but placed following God above pleasing her, even though it would've been good for his career and prevented him from being thrown in prison by her false accusations.
- Job—though surrounded by voices of family and friends telling him what he should believe about his emotional and physical suffering—zeroed in on the voice of God and trusted him above all else.
- Joshua had the courage to obey God's commands, no matter how outlandish they may have sounded to others. By doing so, he was able to lead the way in taking the ancient city of Jericho.
- Jochebed, the mother of Aaron, Miriam, and Moses, went so far as to obey God despite the commands of Pharaoh. She placed her infant son in a basket and sent him floating down the Nile. This not only saved his life but later would help as her people were led out of slavery in Egypt by her then grown-up son.
- The New Testament woman with the issue of blood reached out to touch the hem of Jesus's garment despite what the clamoring crowds thought of her.
- In modern-day times, a sweet senior saint I knew as Ma Schafer recently passed away. As part of her eulogy, her grandson recalled her unpretentious but powerful faith. "Grandma Gerry read her Bible each morning and then closed it, went out, and simply did what it said." I sat there thinking how I, instead, often read the room and then do what others think that I should!

In all these instances, the people purposed to listen to God rather than humans. As someone who has struggled for decades with being controlled by the opinions and expectations of others, I also know it can be done. We learn to do it when we determine to discontinue our chant of *can't*.

I can't tell them the truth for risk of disappointing them.

I can't say no to their request because they are counting on me.

I can't stand up for myself, so I guess I will just acquiesce.

I can't guard my time, even though I know meeting their need is going to stress me right out.

Will you decide today you will begin to conquer your *can't*? God will provide the strength as you run to him rather than bow to others. Sure, it may be stressful for you to stand up for yourself. But either way there is going to be stress. Either you will experience the stress that results from being upfront and honest, risking disappointing, offending, or even angering someone else. Or, you will face the stress of carrying out the wishes of another because you decided to please them rather than do what you sense God is calling you to do.

One prime example of someone who learned to conquer their *can't* is the apostle Peter. In the New Testament narrative, we see him following Jesus from afar, afraid of what others thought (Matthew 26:58; Mark 14:54). He capitulated and lied, and the night Jesus was betrayed, claimed he didn't even know the Lord (Mark 14:70; John 18:25). However, after Jesus's death, resurrection, and ascension into heaven, Peter became emboldened. He stood up for the gospel. He placed pleasing God above pleasing others (Acts 4:12–14). Church tradition even says that when he was put to death in Rome, he requested to be crucified on an inverted cross, not thinking himself worthy to die in the same manner as Jesus did.

If the Lord can take Peter from a place of extreme people pleasing to a life lived so boldly for God, he can do the same for us.

Perfecting the Pivot

My years as a sports reporter—and also as the mother of two basketball players—taught me what the term pivot means when shooting hoops. This is when a player plants one foot firmly on the ground—referred to appropriately as the pivot foot—and then freely moves his or her other foot about in order to reposition himself for passing the basketball or taking a shot. When it comes to pleasing other people, we need to learn to perfect the art of the pivot.

One portion of our desire to please others is noble and praiseworthy. It is even biblical. When we have hearts that love to serve others, we are reflecting the heart of Christ. But without any guardrails in place, our desire to please runs amok.

When we fight against pride and idolatry and properly put God in the driver's seat, we can learn to live a life of service that reflects the gospel to the watching world. As our walk with Christ deepens and strengthens, we will fear less and less what other people think of us or our decisions. We will care most about what God not only thinks of us but what how he desires for us to fill our days. We can still be used to encourage and assist others. Let's just make certain we are being used by God (positive connotation of "used") rather than being used by people (negative connotation of "used").

I try not to overthink all the wrong decisions I've made in the past that were directly related to allowing the opinions and expectations of others rule my life. However, sometimes I do ponder them with this one simple point: how much time I wasted.

I was so busy running around and jumping through everyone else's hoops that I didn't have time to slow down and consult God—through prayer, meditation, and studying his Word, finding out what he thought about the various circumstances and opportunities I faced.

I was so preoccupied with everyone else's opinion of me that I instantly said yes, thereby devoting precious hours of my time each week meeting the needs of someone else without first determining if it was something God wanted me to do.

I was tied up performing tasks and heading up projects that would please church members, fellow sports moms, or even coworkers, often to the detriment of my own family who was just longing for a little down time with a mom who wasn't all frazzled and frenzied.

American founding father Benjamin Franklin was famous for the adage, "Lost time is never found again." It isn't. I can't go back and reclaim those minutes, hours, and even days that I spent spinning my wheels in order to please someone else. You can't either. However, both of us can determine that from this day forward we are not going to let others be the boss of us by their behavior. Instead, we will make our people-pleasing tendencies a serious matter of prayer, asking God to guide us each day, helping us to discern which requests from others we should say yes to and which we shouldn't.

Author J. R. R. Tolkien echoed ol' Ben Franklin when he put these words into the mouth of his character Gandalf in *The Lord of the Rings*: "All we have to decide is what to do with the time that is given us." But before I heard either Ben or J. R. R. make their pronouncements about how we spend our time, there was my friend Debi. I often make important decisions by asking myself a question I once heard her say is a litmus test for her.

When faced with the choice between two activities, she contemplates: "Looking back from the grave, which will I be more thankful that I chose?" This mental framework has really helped to bring clarity to my decision-making process.

Will I be more grateful years from now that I chose to spend time with an aging parent, going out to lunch with them one afternoon, or that I signed up for a third time that year to help with my child's classroom fundraiser?

Will I be thankful I put helping my teary teenage daughter navigate the difficult relationships of middle school above going to a friend's latest product party, so I could make some purchases and help her win bigger hostess prizes?

Will I choose the eternal over the temporary? The essential over the unnecessary? These choices come to us almost daily, sometimes at breakneck speed. The more intentional we are to slow down and not respond before we've prayed, and to ponder what we will think about these decisions years from now, the better equipped we are to make them.

Just a few years ago, actor and former teenage heartthrob David Cassidy—of the singing Partridge family's "I think I love you!" fame—passed away from organ failure at the age of sixty-seven. As has become common in our current culture, his daughter, Katie, took to social media to speak of her father's death and thank those who had offered their condolences and support. In a tweet she wrote,

> Words can't express the solace our family's received from all the love & support during this trying time. My father's last words were "So much wasted time." This will be a daily reminder for me to share my gratitude with those I love as to never waste another minute.... thank you.

So much wasted time.

We aren't given a clue to what Mr. Cassidy was directly referring to. However, the disconcerting sentiment of a man looking back from the grave should be enough to startle us into making choices today that won't find us speaking similar words years from now.

Are you ready to make some life-shifting changes, pivoting in a way that pleases God and loves people, without letting others run your life?

Will you pause before answering, taking the requests of others before the Lord, seeing where *he* stands, before stepping into something that might not be his best plan for you?

Will you dare to speak up rather than give in, when you know you are about to agree to something you undoubtedly shouldn't?

Will you be candid about what your people-pleasing ways are doing to you—both the behavior it produces and the behavior it prevents?

Will you seek to be a person of honesty and integrity, who tactfully and graciously tells the truth rather than one who shades it—even if ever-so-slightly, just to please someone else?

Will you learn to articulate the often hard to pronounce no rather than constantly say yes in order to keep up your competent, capable, or caring image before others?

Are you ready to live an authentic life—one that displays the gospel to a watching world rather than one that seeks to be the savior of anyone within arm's length?

Will you determine *right now* that you will stop making yourself completely miserable by trying to constantly make everyone else happy?

Will you dare to stop putting people in the place of God? He alone is the one we should be striving to please.

He will give you the confidence.

He will allow you to conquer your *can't*.

He will help you live a life that pleases him and is in harmony with others, teaching both you and them important lessons along the way.

He is ready to help you change. Are you ready to cooperate?

You and I can determine to confidently live a no-regret life *starting right now.*

Will you allow me the immense privilege of praying for you?

Father, I lift up to you my stressed-out sister; the one who now holds this book in her hands. Help her to see her immeasurable worth to you. Teach her that she is not solely responsible for the feelings of others, but she is responsible before you for her actions. Grant her boldness when she needs it; tender, yet direct, words when they are necessary. May she learn to manage the tension between pleasing you and relating to others. Help her to make choices she will not regret someday when looking back from the grave. Thank you for the most wonderful example we have in your Son, Jesus. The one who consulted continually with you as he dealt with both people and tasks. May we seek to be more like him both in our devotion to you and our interactions with others. It's in his precious name we pray, Amen.

Acknowledgments

To my agent, Meredith Brock, for your tireless efforts, creative ideas, and willingness to talk while you are out running carpool and I'm home folding laundry.

To Carolyn McCready and my entire Zondervan team, for your commitment to excellence and your encouragement of me and my ministry.

To my Proverbs 31 Ministries family, especially president Lysa TerKeurst, executive director of communications Glynnis Whitwer, and executive director of ministry training Lisa Allen. I love doing ministry with you.

To my online community on social media and through my blog. Connecting with you is both a blessing and a blast! Thank you for your support, encouragement, and ideas.

To my prayer team made up of ninety-three fabulous women, for hitting your knees on my behalf. I couldn't—and wouldn't want to—do this without you.

To my remarkable assistants, Kim Stewart and Dana Herndon, for your heartfelt support, magnificent skills, and fast turnaround times!

To friends Nicki Koziarz, Ruth Schwenk, and Courtney Joseph, for always being only a Voxer message away.

To my mother, Margaret Patterson, who unexpectedly passed

away just as I was finishing this book, for loving God, me, and our entire family so well.

To my family, husband Todd and children Kenna, Jason, Mitchell, Macey, and Spencer—three of whom are biological and two who are by marriage, but I forget which ones are which. I love processing life with you and laughing at our zany family text threads.

To Jesus, for taking my place on the cross and offering me a forever home in heaven. Indescribable.

Resources

For Dealing with a Narcissist

If you are in a relationship with a truly narcissistic person, I strongly suggest you seek out a Christian counselor in your area by visiting ccn.thedirectorywidget.com. Additionally, a helpful resource is *Understanding and Loving a Person with Narcissistic Personality Disorder: Biblical and Practical Wisdom to Build Empathy, Preserve Boundaries, and Show Compassion* (The Arterburn Wellness Series) by Steve Arterburn, David C. Cook Publisher, copyright 2018.

Personality Type Resources

Discovering and exploring our unique personality blends can be key to understanding some deeper reasons that we people-please. Start with any of these practical books to learn more about your distinctive temperament:

Wired That Way Personality Profile: An Easy-to-Use Questionnaire for Helping You Discover Your God-Given Personality Type by Marita Littauer and Florence Littauer, Revell Publishers, copyright 2019
The Sacred Enneagram: Finding Your Unique Path to Spiritual Growth by Christopher L. Heuertz, Zondervan Publishers, copyright 2017

The Road Back to You: An Enneagram Journey to Self-Discovery by Ian
  Morgan Cron and Suzanne Stabile, IVP Books, copyright 2016
The Path Between Us: An Enneagram Journey to Healthy Relationships
  by Suzanne Stabile, IVP Books, copyright 2018
Gifts Differing: Understanding Personality Type, 2nd ed., by Isabel
  Briggs Myers and Peter B. Myers, Davies-Black Publishing, a
  division of CCP, Inc., copyright 1995

Seven "Stop It!" Statements for People Pleasers

Here are some go-to phrases for you to ponder, and even commit to memory if you would like. They will help you realign your thinking when you start to wander down the path of people pleasing. They are ready to be photocopied, cut out, and placed where they will be seen often, such as the kitchen sink, bathroom mirror, or vehicle dashboard.

Every *need* is not necessarily your *call*.

Don't take on more than you can *pray* for.

Their *happiness* is
not your assignment.

You don't need their
permission
to do God's will.

Stop making *their* feelings
your responsibility.

You don't owe them an *excuse*
for why you said no, but you
will owe *God* an explanation
for why you said *yes*.

You can still say *yes*
to the friendship while saying
no to a friend.

Truth Bombs for
Memorization

For your convenience, here again are the verses from chapter four on being truthful. They have been designed for photocopying and cutting out to keep in a prominent place such as your car dashboard, the kitchen sink, a bathroom mirror, or even in an envelope in your purse.

> "*Do not lie to each other, since you have taken off your old self with its practices and have put on the new self, which is being renewed in knowledge in the image of its Creator*" (COLOSSIANS 3:9–10).

> "*Therefore each of you must put off falsehood and speak truthfully to your neighbor, for we are all members of one body*" (EPHESIANS 4:25).

> "*LORD, who may dwell in your sacred tent? Who may live on your holy mountain? The one whose walk is blameless, who does what is righteous, who speaks the truth from their heart*" (PSALM 15:1–2).

"*Instead*, speaking the truth in love, we will grow to become in every respect the mature body of him who is the head, that is, Christ" (EPHESIANS 4:15).

"*Lying lips* are detestable to the LORD, but faithful people are his delight" (PROVERBS 12:22 CSB).

"*I know*, my God, that you test the heart and are pleased with integrity" (1 CHRONICLES 29:17).

"*Truthful words* stand the test of time, but lies are soon exposed" (PROVERBS 12:19 NLT).

"*These* are the things you must do: Speak truth to one another; make true and sound decisions within your city gates" (ZECHARIAH 8:16 CSB).

"*Whoever* of you loves life and desires to see many good days, keep your tongue from evil and your lips from telling lies. Turn from evil and do good; seek peace and pursue it. The eyes of the LORD are on the righteous, and his ears are attentive to their cry" (PSALM 34:12–15).

"*There* are six things the LORD hates, seven that are detestable to him: haughty eyes, a lying tongue, hands that shed innocent blood, a heart that devises wicked schemes, feet that are quick to rush into evil, a false witness who pours out lies and a person who stirs up conflict in the community" (PROVERBS 6:16–19).

About the Author

Karen Ehman is a *New York Times* bestselling author, a Proverbs 31 Ministries speaker, and a writer for *Encouragement for Today*, an online devotional that reaches over four million users daily. She has written seventeen books and Bible studies and is a contributing writer for the First 5 Bible study app. Karen has been featured on numerous media outlets including *TODAY Show Parents*, FoxNews.com, Redbook.com, Crosswalk.com, and *HomeLife Magazine*. Her passion is to help women live their priorities as they reflect the gospel to a watching world. Married to her college sweetheart, Todd, the mother of three and mother-in-law of two, she enjoys collecting vintage Pyrex kitchenware, cheering for the Detroit Tigers, and feeding the many people who gather around her mid-century dining room table for a taste of Mama Karen's cooking. Connect with her at karenehman.com.

Proverbs 31
MINISTRIES

Know the Truth. Live the Truth. It changes everything.

If you were inspired by Karen Ehman's *When Making Others Happy Is Making You Miserable* and desire to deepen your own personal relationship with Jesus Christ, Proverbs 31 Ministries has just what you are looking for.

Proverbs 31 Ministries exists to be a trusted friend who will take you by the hand and walk by your side, leading you one step closer to the heart of God through:

- Free online daily devotions
- First 5 Bible study app
- Online Bible studies
- Podcast
- COMPEL writer training
- She Speaks Conference
- Books and resources

Our desire is to help you to know the Truth and live the Truth. Because when you do, it changes everything.

For more information about Proverbs 31 Ministries, visit: www.Proverbs31.org.

Notes

Chapter 1: The Prison of People Pleasing

1. IMPORTANT NOTE: This book was written with the average person in mind who deals with the normal feelings and pressure to please others. If you are dealing with a more serious issue such as verbal abuse or actual physical harm, get help! Reach out to your pastor, if you have one. Or you can find a Christian counselor in your area by visiting ccn.thedirectorywidget.com. Or, if you are in physical danger and being abused, *please* stop what you are doing now and call the National Domestic Violence Hotline at 1–800–799–7233 or visit http://www.thehotline.org/.

Chapter 2: What (Or Actually Who) Are We Afraid Of?

1. https://www.merriam-webster.com/dictionary/addiction
2. https://www.psychologytoday.com/ie/basics/dopamine

Chapter 3: Pushers, Pouters, Guilt Bombers, and Others Who Try to Call the Shots

1. Edward Welch, *When People Are Big and God Is Small* (Phillipsburg, NJ: P&R Publishing, 1997), 181.
2. https://apologetics315.com/2013/02/charles-spurgeon-on-discernment/

Chapter 4: Well, to Be Honest with You

1. https://www.usip.org/publications/2011/11/handling-conflict-peaceful-means

Chapter 5: What Digital Is Doing to Us

1. https://www.textrequest.com/blog/texting-statistics-answer-questions/
2. https://blog.htc.ca/2013/05/27/response-time-expectations-in-the-internet-age-how-long-is-too-long/

Chapter 6: How to Be in the "No"

1. Lysa TerKeurst, *The Best Yes: Making Wise Decisions in the Midst of Endless Demands* (Nashville: Thomas Nelson, 2014), 189.
2. https://www.psychologytoday.com/us/blog/stretching-theory/201809/how-many-decisions-do-we-make-each-day

Chapter 7: It's Not about You (But Sometimes It Should Be)

1. https://www.christianitytoday.com/ct/2019/august-web-only/virtue-vice-why-niceness-weakens-our-witness.html
2. https://www.medicaldaily.com/people-pleaser-brain-activity-mental-stress-376139
3. Sharon Hodde Mille, *Nice: Why We Love to Be Liked and How God Calls Us to More* (Grand Rapids: Baker Books, 2019), 17.
4. Henry Cloud and John Townsend, *Boundaries: When to Say Yes, How to Say No to Take Control of Your Life* (Grand Rapids: Zondervan, 2017), 249–250.
5. https://parade.com/1074817/allymeyerowitz/eleanor-roosevelt-quote/

Chapter 8: The Juggle Is Real

1. Lysa TerKeurst, *The Best Yes: Making Wise Decisions in the Midst of Endless Demands* (Nashville: Thomas Nelson, 2014), 27.

Chapter 9: It All Comes Down to You and Jesus

1. https://www.christianquotes.info/quotes-by-author/dwight-l-moody-quotes/

New Video Study for Your Church or Small Group

If you've enjoyed this book, now you can go deeper with the companion video Bible study!

In this six-session study, Karen Ehman helps you apply the principles in *When Making Others Happy Is Making You Miserable* to your life. The study guide includes streaming video access, video teaching notes, group discussion questions, personal reflection questions, and a leader's guide.

Study Guide with
Streaming Video
9780310082767

DVD
9780310082781

Available January 2022 at your favorite bookstore,
or streaming video on StudyGateway.com.

Keep Showing Up

How to Stay Crazy in Love When Your Love Drives You Crazy

Karen Ehman, New York Times *bestselling author*

It is true that opposites attract–for a while. But often as the years go by in our marriages, opposites may also begin to attack. The habits and characteristics we once found endearing about our significant other are the exact things that drive us crazy years later!

Whether you and your spouse disagree about finances, parenting, or how to load the dishwasher, your differences don't need to divide you. They can actually bring you closer together—and closer to God.

In *Keep Showing Up*, Karen Ehman will help you to . . .

- Play to each other's strengths as you work on your own weaknesses
- Become a faithful forgiver who also forgets
- Discover strategies for avoiding the social media comparison trap
- Resist the dangerous tendency to mimic a friend's marriage
- Unearth the magic in the midst of the mundane
- Experience how a spouse who drives you crazy can drive you straight to Jesus

Throughout *Keep Showing Up*, Karen includes ideas to strengthen your marriage right now, such as how to find your calling as a couple, date-night discussion starters, and tips for rediscovering romance in the midst of the routine. Learn how your "incompatibility" can actually become the strength of your marital team in this real-life guide to both living with and loving your spouse—differences and all.

Available in stores and online!

ZONDERVAN®
.com

Listen, Love, Repeat

Other-Centered Living in a Self-Centered World

Karen Ehman, New York Times *bestselling author*

Our culture is obsessed with self. In our schedules, our relationships, and especially online. But we are less content than in decades past. The reason? We have forgotten the joy that comes from putting others first.

Reclaiming that joy requires us to live alert, listening for "heart drops"—hints from those in our lives who might need a helping hand or a generous dose of encouragement.

Listen, Love, Repeat gives practical, creative ways to scatter kindness, including loving our family and friends, reaching out to the lonely, blessing the "necessary people" who help us get life done every day, and loving the hard-to-love.

As we share love, we create a safe space where we can openly share the gospel with others. And we get to see lives changed right before our very eyes—not only the lives of others, but our lives as well. It's as easy as one, two, three.

Listen. Love. And then? Repeat.

Available in stores and online!

Hoodwinked

Ten Myths Moms Believe & Why We All Need to Knock It Off

Karen Ehman and Ruth Schwenk

Moms have been hoodwinked—tricked into believing lies that keep them from not only enjoying motherhood but forging friendships with other moms who might tackle the tasks of motherhood differently. Myths such as "Mothering is natural, easy, and instinctive" cause moms to feel like failures if they have questions or apprehensions in raising their kids. Operating from the premise that "The way I mother is the right (and only) way" puts up fences between moms instead of building bridges of encouragement between them. Lies such as "I am my child's choices" tempt moms to mistakenly believe that if their child makes a wrong choice then they, in turn, must be a bad mom.

In their encouraging "we've been there" style, Karen Ehman and Ruth Schwenk enable mothers to:

- Identify ten myths of motherhood
- Replace the lies with the truth of what God says
- Acquire practical tools to help them form new and improved thought patterns and healthy behaviors
- Forge healthy, supportive relationships with other moms of all ages and stages
- Confidently embrace the calling of motherhood as they care for their families in their own unique way

Six-session DVD study also available.

Available in stores and online!

ZONDERVAN®
.com

Keep It Shut

What to Say, How to Say It, and When to Say Nothing at All

Karen Ehman, New York Times *bestselling author*

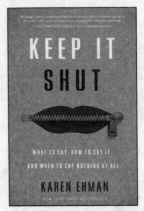

From Bible times to modern times, women have struggled with their words. What to say and how to say it. What not to say. When it is best to remain silent. And what to do when you've said something you wish you could now take back. In this book a woman whose mouth has gotten her into loads of trouble shares the hows (and how-not-tos) of dealing with the tongue.

Beyond just a "how not to gossip" book, this book explores what the Bible says about the many ways we are to use our words and the times when we are to remain silent. Karen will cover using our speech to interact with friends, coworkers, family, and strangers as well as in the many places we use our words in private, in public, online, and in prayer. Even the words we say silently to ourselves. She will address unsolicited opinion-slinging, speaking the truth in love, not saying words just to people-please, and dealing with our verbal anger.

Christian women struggle with their mouths. Even though we know that Scripture has much to say about how we are—and are not—to use our words, this is still an immense issue, causing heartache and strain not only in family relationships, but also in friendships, work, and church settings.

Available in stores and online!

Let. It. Go.

How to Stop Running the Show and Start Walking in Faith

Karen Ehman, New York Times *bestselling author*

Doable ideas, thought patterns, and tools to help you LET GO OF YOUR NEED TO CONTROL

The housework. The meals. The kids. Many women are wired to control. But trying to control everything can be exhausting, and it can also cause friction with your friends and family.

This humorous yet thought-provoking book guides you as you discover the freedom and reward of living a life "out of control," in which you allow God to be seated in the rightful place in your life. Armed with relevant biblical and current examples (both to emulate and to avoid), doable ideas, new thought patterns, and practical tools to implement, *Let. It. Go.* will gently lead you out of the land of over control into a place of quiet trust.

A companion video-based study for small groups is also available.

Available in stores and online!